Sue ;
From

Forks in the Road

by James Edward Alexander

James Edward Alexander
1/22/14

Forks

In

The Road

A Journey Charted by God and the Library of Congress

James Edward Alexander

Also by James Edward Alexander

Half way Home From Kinderlou (2008)

If I Should Die Before I Wake ... What Happens to My Stuff? (2009)

For information about permission to reproduce selections from this book,
write to JEA Trilogy, P.O. Box 2809, Bluffton, SC 29910

**Personalized autographed copies of all books by James Edward
Alexander can be purchased at** www.jeatrilogy.com

ISBN: **978-0-9850359-0-7**

Cover illustrated by

Barbara McArtor

mcart@charter.net

Dedications:

To Judy Alexander, who, as wife and mother of our four children, helped shape significant sign posts along this passage.

To James Christopher, Joycelyn Louise, Kenneth Anthony, and Dorothea Marie; our children, whose love and support continue to stoke the fires that fuel my wonderful life

***

To Toian Bowser-Alexander, my wife, who provides comfort and support for me to remember and record what happened.

***

To John Briley, and Wilson Brydon, who directed me to forks in the road that guided me to this day.

***

To my heroes -- my adult neighbors in my childhood, many of whom had little, if any, formal education.

At the age of seven, one of them gave me this advice:

> "What you is is what you think you is,
> So make yourself what you wanna be."

His gift instructs that I am who I am by my own appraisal and definition. And, if I don't like who I am, it is my responsibility to change myself. Thus, never forfeit to another person the right to label my identity or to solely guide my destiny.

***

Special Acknowledgments

Franklin Williams and Harold Duane Gunnerud

For more than 50 years I searched for a group picture of my basic training unit, taken at Lackland Air Force Base in 1951. In 2010, Franklin Williams, with whom I shared high school and the same date of enlistment in the Air Force, searched his military records and found a personnel roster of Flight #1607. He served for 26 years. That document was also the Order promoting us to the rank of PFC. Armed with that roster I searched internet telephone directories and contacted Harold D. Gunnerud, who promptly remembered me and gave me his original copy of the group picture, which he had preserved for 58 years 8 months. Franklin Williams died April 26, 2011.

***

Research support and special photographs were supplied by The 37th Training Wing History Office, Lackland AFB, TX

CONTENTS

Chapter Five: THE OLD WORLD AND A NEW DIRECTION

Chapter Six: ROLL THE DICE; SOMETIMES YOU WIN

Chapter Seven: NEW VISIONS ON THE HORIZON

Introduction

This is volume II of memories of a wonderful life. In volume I, *Half Way Home From Kinderlou*, published in 2008, I shared some pleasant memories before my teen years in Valdosta, Georgia.

Teen ages are that interlude between childhood and adulthood; a period of simultaneous rapid growth and decline, when there is so much more to learn, while forgetting the habits of kindergarten. Teen ages are the days when parents and the community subject youthful behavior to closer scrutiny, looking for confirmation of what should have been learned after they excused childish missteps as innocent or "cute."

In that period of youthful sunshine I spent much of my excess energy as the high school quarterback, playing semi-pro baseball and learning why my body suddenly felt different in the presence of girls.

After school and on Saturday, I continued to work in a variety of jobs, but as I approached graduation from high school, four episodes signaled that my future was beyond the socioeconomic boundary of Valdosta, and that I would have to chart new courses on roads not yet travelled.

Chapter One: PUTTING AWAY CHILDISH THINGS

Advice

Motorists travelling south through Valdosta on U.S. highway 41 in the late 1940s could stop at the ABC package store and buy store-bought liquor. Adjacent to that store was a drive-in restaurant where white travelers could park and order beer and a hamburger. On Saturdays, I was their waiter.

My job as a 15-year-old car hop often included more than adjusting the food-and-beer-laden metal tray on side windows. Sometimes, I was asked by the riders in one car to keep my eyes open for the arrival of another car, and to keep my mouth shut about what happened when the occupants of both cars gathered into one vehicle. My vigilance and silence was worth a quarter. Some days I made an extra dollar in hush money.

One day in 1950, two young white University of Florida students stopped for refreshments. They were en route home after attending the Georgia-Florida football game. When they said their hometown was St. Petersburg, I told them of my pending visit to that city on Christmas day to challenge the all-colored Gibbs High School Gladiators. As they departed, they expressed anticipation of my visit.

Our friendly exchange was observed by the liquor store clerk, who approached me and said, "Boy, you ought to forget about attending college when you're done with high school. Don't try to be no lawyer or doctor. You're a nigger boy, and you'll do just fine if you just keep your wits and don't try to overdo it. Go out yonder and get yourself a good job at the mill. Forget about being too uppity. You'll be happier that way."

His words were also heard by Mister Rich, the owner of the store, a soft spoken gentleman, whose warmth was expressed in his pleasant and gentle smile. He ushered me to a quieter space and also offered advice. In an obvious reference to his clerk, he said, "You know, James Edward, some men lack drive and vision, and they try to discourage their opposites from succeeding. He knows you are a clever youngster." Then he put his arm on my shoulder and concluded, "James Edward, you can be anything you want to be, or do anything anybody else can do, as long as you're willing to work for it. I've got a feeling you'll make good choices. I wish you the very best."

As I walked home I heard the echoes of his advice, offered in a different, though eloquent tongue: "What you is, is what you think you is, So make yourself what you wanna be."

The Funeral

During my childhood in Valdosta, funerals were regularly scheduled at churches on Sunday, almost immediately following the morning services. It was a sensible arrangement, since mourners already had on their Sunday-go-to-meeting clothes, and "meeting" included funerals. Furthermore, Sunday funerals were convenient for folks who couldn't miss a day of work during the week. One Sunday they met to say farewell to Joe.

In the interlude between the regular service and the funeral, Gussie walked a block back to her home and changed clothes. When she returned she wore, not the dark colors of bereavement, but something that suggested her relationship with the departed. --- a bright red dress. Her light green hat was perfectly tilted to hide the full expressions of her eyes. Gussie came to the funeral to say goodbye, and to say a few other things that were on her mind. She took a seat in the last unoccupied pew, creating for herself a little zone of privacy. She was unaware that I stood in a nook behind her, in my assigned place as a member of the funeral home staff.

Joe was a young man, like so many other colored men who died before fifty candles marked their history. That troubled me, because I reckoned that some of them might still be alive if they had received different medical care. There were no colored doctors in Valdosta. Although I never heard any complaints about the care white doctors gave colored patients, I pondered how I might become a doctor, to live among and care for my neighbors. I also knew it would take a long time to become a doctor, but I had more time than Joe.

Sometimes funerals are assemblies in which the living make excuses for the dead and occasionally even attempt to dignify a less praiseworthy existence. My elders rationalized this practice: "Don't speak ill of the dead; the devil might be listening." The minister honored this tradition. His first words of the eulogy caused Gussie to stir. She shifted and tried to make herself comfortable, anticipating that what she was about to hear was what the congregation knew, or thought they knew. She knew some things that were at one time privy to only three persons: herself, Joe, and God. It was not a particularly warm day, but her body temperature was her business, and she regulated it as best she could with the hand held cardboard fan with the picture of Mahalia Jackson on the front and the name of the funeral home which donated it to the church on the back.

When the minister announced, "Brother Joe was a good man," Gussie shifted and grunted, the kind of noise that often signals suspicion and disagreement.

Then, she twitched her heavily painted lips, and uttered in a hushed voice: "He was good for only one thing, but that ain't what killed him."

The minister continued. "He was a faithful and honest servant, a giving man, ready, if necessary, to give you the shirt off his back in your hour of need. Let the church say amen."

Gussie's only response was a more audible "Lawd, Lawd." The chorus of amen's continued, but Gussie was having her own private talk with Joe. She knew he could still hear her voice, just as he had in those private and special places where they made their own record.

When all the tributes had been paid and the crying and moaning ceased, the pallbearers took their positions. But Gussie had one final message.

Some years later I learned that what she expressed was called ambivalence – the simultaneous conflicting feelings toward a person, as love and hate. She leaned forward, as though God was seated directly in front of her, and she said. "Now God, you know I ain't gonna lie to you, so here's what's on my mind. If he showed you something that he didn't show me, then you deal with it as you see fit." She hesitated and cleared her throat, as to make sure her words were not misunderstood, not even by God, to whom she added, "As for me, God, I'd appreciate it if we don't end up in the same place, 'cause I don't ever want to see his tired, lying, trifling ass again --- in this world or the next. Amen." She then fanned a little faster and hummed a tune.

When the pall bearers rolled Joe's coffin past her, she smiled and said, "Bye honey."

Boy, Are You Old Enough To Drink?

At age 15 my reputation as a diligent worker spread quickly among my mother's white employers. One day as I walked with my hand-powered lawn mower to another yard cleaning job, a truck pulled along side me and the white driver stopped and asked: "Are you James Edward?" When I answered affirmatively, he introduced himself as Mister Ferguson. We sat in his truck, and he offered me another job cleaning many of the windows in the downtown stores. He was an extremely polite man who reported that he was making me this offer because of my reputation as a hard working, honest young fellow. Then he explained his proposal, in terms which carefully emphasized my prerogatives to accept or reject.

He would furnish the window washing equipment – pails, squeegees, cloths, soaps, etc. I would clean approximately 40 windows at least twice per month, and be paid $1.00 per window per month. We parted company while I pondered his proposal for a few days. Within the week we met again; I accepted his offer, and promptly began making my rounds.

It was a pleasant job. All of the windows were at businesses owned and operated by white merchants. One large window was in a bar, for white customers only. Whenever I entered to fill my water pail, the bartender jokingly asked, "Boy, are you old enough to drink?" At age 15, I always answered, "No sir, not yet." His customers were always the same; men who spent most of their

15

days drinking cheap whiskey and chain-smoking Lucky Strikes, Camels, and Chesterfield cigarettes. They never insulted me. One day that changed.

Immediately upon entering the tavern, a new customer challenged my presence. He was already drunk, and smelled as if he had wallowed with swine -- before the swine evicted him. Before the bartender could get his attention to validate my purpose, the drunkard swiftly kicked me in the butt. There was a noticeable silence among the other patrons, but my offender laughed loudly. Then he approached me again, staggering and trying to steady his body for another kick. My own instincts kicked in, prompting me to grab his filthy shirt and guide his head through the glass door. Then, without further ado, I walked over his sprawled body and went directly to the police station and reported what happened. One officer, a regular customer at the drive-in restaurant where I also worked on Saturday, knew my temperament and that I was unlikely to attack a white man without serious provocation. He walked with me to the bar. Another officer drove the patrol car to the scene.

We entered and saw a bloated, stinking, bloody man still sitting in the middle of shattered glass. His explanation was preempted by another patron who told the officers: "That boy didn't sass or provoke that fellow, but the fellow did kick the boy's ass, then the boy was trying to get out of the way of another ass kicking when that fellow slipped and fell head first through the glass." Then, he looked around the bar and asked aloud, "Ain't that what you fellows saw?" There was consensus. His lie probably saved my life that day, but I could not build a future on such unpredictable generosity.

One policeman leaned over to check the man's wounds, but the odor disgusted him. The other officer ordered the man to get up and get ready to follow them to the jail. But the officer quickly realized that the stench would foul their workplace, so he simply ordered the man to get up and find his way to the other side of the city limit sign. Mister Ferguson was notified, and he came in haste to stand at my side and to replace the glass.

My mother never heard what happened that day. It was just one of those events among males, this time, coincidently involving white men, a hard working respectful colored boy, and a disgusting outsider who threatened the peace of our community. After the event, the bartender asked, "Boy, you sure you don't need a drink?"

A New Word for Survival

Mrs. Chauncey, one of my favorite white employers, was an old lady who was determined to wring the last ounce of energy from her small frail body. She exerted most of her pep in her yard, tending to camellias, azaleas, hibiscus, pansies, and roses.

After working about two hours on the first day, she asked how much she owed me. When I told her I generally charged by the entire day, she promptly asked for my hourly rate and reminded me that I was the only person who should put a value on my labor. After setting my price, she opened a wooden cigar box; removed a very large handgun, and counted out my wages.

Our relationship was marked by paying close attention to each other and trading gestures that signaled mutual respect. If she pricked her finger on a rose thorn, I would go in the house, pretending to get a drink of water, but my real purpose was to soak a little alcohol on a cloth and bring it to her to dab her wound, thus confirming my attention and concern. Likewise, she could sense when I really needed a cool drink, and she would go inside and prepare lemonade, and we would sit and sip together.

Although I didn't have a regular schedule, she soon noticed that Wednesday afternoon became my preference. Then she also noticed why. Between 3:45 and 4:00 O'clock, I positioned myself to work near the sidewalk, where a very attractive white girl would pass on her way from school. At first we casually recognized each

18

other, which ripened into a wave, then we spoke to each other, and then we anticipated each other's presence. Mrs. Chauncey watched the pattern developing. One Wednesday the sweltering temperature also gave Mrs. Chauncey an excuse to temporarily stop pruning and do something different. As I positioned myself near the front, she joined me. When the girl appeared, almost trotting to an expected rendezvous, Mrs. Chauncey promptly offered the girl and me a glass of lemonade, and then escorted us to the rear of the house, which was shielded by large hedges. After pouring three glasses of refreshment, the old lady pretended to hear the telephone and excused herself. Ten minutes later she returned; complimented the girl on how well she maintained her auburn hair, and signaled the end of the session.

Later, as Mrs. Chauncey tended to our business with the cigar box, she told me about a man and a woman whose public display of affection caused a stir in the community. She said they were not *discrete,* and she cautioned, "James Edward, remember the word *discretion.*" On that day she sent me home with something extra: the wisdom of an elder, and a new word for survival.

Calling the Right Play

Even as we huddled on our opponent's 40 yard line, my attention was divided between the next play and the path I would take after graduation. I addressed both. My first call: "Ok guys, when we graduate next May, I'm going into the Air Force. Who wants to go with me?" Franklin Williams said, "Ok, I'll go with you, but what's the play gonna be?" We heard a whistle that signaled delay of game. Coach Smith called me to the sideline and asked for an explanation. I told him I had observed their left cornerback limping and that I wanted to make sure we could take advantage of his disability. He knew I was lying, but when I returned to the new huddle, I gave Nolan Williams specific instructions: "Fake an inside route, then go straight to the end zone corner. Don't look back until you get to the goal line, then look over your shoulder. The ball will fall in your arms." After the five yard penalty, I took the snap and faded 10 yards. The next day the sports section of the Valdosta Daily Times reported that Williams received a 55 yard touchdown pass from Alexander in the waning minutes to claim victory. Somewhere my guardian angel also made a notation: James Edward owes me --- another one.

Since the age of 10 I had worked in tobacco fields, cleaned yards, harvested pecans, delivered newspapers, shined shoes, delivered clothing for a men's clothing store, delivered furniture, worked as a funeral home assistant, helped white women with their gardens and spring cleaning, gathered moss from oak trees, washed windows, and served as a car hop at a drive-in restaurant where I also doubled as a lookout for people who met other people where neither should have been and did what neither should have done. I did not have money for college, but what I really needed was new lines of work -- in different places.

Chapter Two: MAMA, IT'S TIME TO GO

Searching for a Place to Become a Man

On the evening of my visit to the local armed forces recruiter I asked for my mother's permission to join the Air Force when I reached the minimum age. When I started to explain that there were things I wanted to do that couldn't be done in Valdosta, she interrupted me and recited my grand papa's observation: "The things you do when you don't have to will determine who you will be when you can't help it." She granted my request with her signature, a prerequisite for me to enlist at age 17.

On July 26, 1947, almost four years before I enlisted, President Harry S. Truman signed the National Security Act of 1947, to create new intelligence and military agencies to streamline our national defense posture. That Act established the Central Intelligence Agency, the National Security Council, the U.S. Air Force as a separate military branch, and structured all military services under a Secretary of Defense. Exactly one year later The Commander-In-Chief signed what I consider one of the most important documents ever signed by any President: *Executive Order 9981* ended racial segregation in the armed forces of the United States. That Order ultimately altered American, and indeed worldwide, social and economic patterns. When colored men and white men were forced to change their behavior in the armed forces - the most representative   cross section of the population at that time - they talked with each other at different volume levels and inflection and erased another barrier to understanding and mutual respect.

It was into this setting that I, a colored child from the Deep South, entered to become a man.

Executive Order 9981

Establishing the President's Committee on Equality of Treatment and Opportunity In the Armed Forces.

WHEREAS it is essential that there be maintained in the armed services of the United States the highest standards of democracy, with equality of treatment and opportunity for all those who serve in our country's defense:

NOW THEREFORE, by virtue of the authority vested in me as President of the United States, by the Constitution and the statutes of the United States, and as Commander in Chief of the armed services, it is hereby ordered as follows:

1. It is hereby declared to be the policy of the President that there shall be equality of treatment and opportunity for all persons in the armed services without regard to race, color, religion or national origin. This policy shall be put into effect as rapidly as possible, having due regard to the time required to effectuate any necessary changes without impairing efficiency or morale.

2. There shall be created in the National Military Establishment an advisory committee to be known as the President's Committee on Equality of Treatment and Opportunity in the Armed Services, which shall be composed of seven members to be designated by the President.

3. The Committee is authorized on behalf of the President to examine into the rules, procedures and practices of the Armed Services in order to determine in what respect such rules, procedures and practices may be altered or improved with a view to carrying out the policy of this order. The Committee shall confer and advise the Secretary of Defense, the Secretary of the Army, the Secretary of the Navy, and the Secretary of the Air Force, and shall make such recommendations to the President and to said

Secretaries as in the judgment of the Committee will effectuate the policy hereof.

4. All executive departments and agencies of the Federal Government are authorized and directed to cooperate with the Committee in its work, and to furnish the Committee such information or the services of such persons as the Committee may require in the performance of its duties.

5. When requested by the Committee to do so, persons in the armed services or in any of the executive departments and agencies of the Federal Government shall testify before the Committee and shall make available for use of the Committee such documents and other information as the Committee may require.

6. The Committee shall continue to exist until such time as the President shall terminate its existence by Executive order.

Harry Truman
The White House
July 26, 1948

We Knew Our Destination, But Not our Fate

Each step I took in the direction of the Trailways Bus station repeated so many walks downtown. Although time would eventually erase my footprints, wherever I would wander, the new place would only be my residence; Valdosta would always be my home.

Sergeant Bandy, the recruiter, waited at the bus station to say goodbye to the nine colored enlistees. Another contingent of white recruits waited in a separate room. We all knew our destination but not our fate. Bandy took his position at the door of the bus, beneath the sign in the rectangular window above the windshield which read "Chartered." He was smartly dressed in his Army uniform with a clipboard in hand. His instructions were clear: "Now y'all listen up. When I call your last name, first name, and middle initial, I want you to get aboard this here bus and take a seat. You will keep that seat until somebody at the Armed Forces Induction Center in Columbus, Georgia, tells you to get up and get off." He yelled, "Alexander, James E." I stepped forward and made my way down the aisle and took a seat near the rear of the bus -- just as I always did on a common carrier carrying colored and white passengers. In turn, Baldwin, Carmichael, Duncan, Jenkins, McCaskill, McCloud, Plummer, and Williams, took seats near me. As we traveled in the direction of my home on U.S. Highway 84, my seat gave me a clear view to wave another

26

goodbye to my mother who waited in the yard to watch my departure. As a child I had ridden the Trailways bus to and from the rural community of Ousley more times than I could remember. This time when I passed my usual stop at the junction of the paved highway and the long dirt country road, I sensed that my childhood was over.

There wasn't much conversation on our ride to Columbus. Each man seemed to be contemplating his own future. Approximately four hours later we were greeted by another sergeant at the center where all military recruits assembled, regardless of branch of service. We assembled in a large room and were introduced to military forms which requested information on almost everything I did since I first played hop scotch, and on almost every relative, living or dead. Then we were introduced to military food, an assortment of edibles piled on a metal tray with indented spaces.

Our next gathering was in another room lined with beds, one on top of the other. Somebody called them bunk beds. I knew a regular bed that I shared every night with my brother, sister, and at least one cousin, and I knew how to arrange a floor pallet. I did not know bunk beds. Our schedule for tomorrow included mental and physical exams, and they wanted us to be alert, so a sergeant with a lot of stripes on his sleeves told us the lights would go out at 10 p.m. At 9:45 he reminded us that we had 15, not 16, minutes left. That was enough time for each man to ponder what must be

27

pondered when you rest your head for the night in a strange bed. Those of us from the same town tried to get bunks close together, probably acting on that impulse to be close to something familiar when you wade into a stream of uncertainty. We also called each person's name to further signal the number of one's allies in a congregation of strangers.

The sergeant re-appeared to say goodnight. He seemed to have synchronized his watch with the light switch. At precisely 10 p.m., the room was dark and quiet.

Open Wide --- Everything

At precisely 5:00 a.m., 22, 1951, the lights were turned on, illuminating both the room and the path to my future. Those western movies depicting cattle drives pale in comparison to the pace with which we were herded through stalls for physical examinations. Our roundup began promptly after breakfast. Lines were formed, each comprising approximately 25 men.

We stood at the entrance to a large building, mindful of the sergeant's plain directive: obey the medics and no talking, except to answer their questions. Doctors, nurses, and technicians opened the gates as other sergeants kept the stream of bodies flowing. Their technique was to literally strip everything and everybody to the bare bottom line. There were shiny asses a-plenty.

I had been in a doctor's office only three times in my life, but was not required to undress during any visit. But these medics were trying to determine our fitness for military service, and they knew exactly what they needed to see and where to find it. We examinees moved to the rhythm of an incessant chorus of instructions: hold this straight, bend that, raise arms, lift feet, turn left, squat right, cough, and open wide - everything. One pair of hands checked the muscle tone of my neck and upper extremities, other fingers found my middle, front, and behind, leaving me befuddled. They used an assortment of gauges, scopes, mirrors, rubber hammers, scales, tubes, needles, bottles, and other instruments to get what they wanted. Everything they used was cold. It was an ignoble spectacle. But, there was a war being fought in Korea, and the pipeline to the fronts needed a steady flow of bodies. No time to tarry.

As each man finished the examination, he was directed to another large room where he selected a seat next to another man who had just completed the common experience. Now we were a salt-and-pepper multitude, comprising a mixture of races, ethnicities, habits and expectations that each man brought from towns and cities throughout Georgia, Florida, and Alabama. Having to look past calm white faces to get Franklin Williams' attention evoked strange emotions. He and I could feel a change coming.

A Pair of Aces

By the third day the most important change in our vocabulary was the way we cited the time of day. I didn't yet know why, but military time is given in four numbers. So, instead of getting up at 4:30 a.m., we were roused out of our beds at 0430, and before the minute hand made a full circle, we had cleared linen from our bunks, eaten breakfast, and formed a ragged formation for the march to waiting buses.

Less than 12 hours earlier I raised my hand and took the oath of enlistment, promising, as I had done as a Boy Scout, to do my best. Almost three years after Executive Order 9981 was signed, we newly-inducted Southern boys marched to the waiting troop train in separate racial formations. One sergeant commanded: "You white fellows fall in over here, you colored boys fall in over yonder." Another sergeant stood at the train entrance with his roster and clipboard and ordered each new recruit to board and yell his last name, first name, middle initial, and the newly assigned serial number.

"Alexander, James Edward, AF14417061," I reported and stepped forward. That was my first violation of a military command. The sergeant told me so.

"Dammit boy, I didn't ask for your whole horsepower (entire name). I said middle initial, what's this James Edward crap?"

Shaking, I responded, "But that's what my mama named me - sir." The U.S. Government had just given me a number with eight digits to wear around for the next four years, and had just restricted the other five letters of my name which I carried for 17 years.

Our train waited on side tracks to transport new airmen to Texas and a contingent of sailors and marines to Memphis and California. A slender colored airman, a graduate of the all-Negro Ft. Valley State College, was charged with supervising the activities and conduct of colored troops aboard the train. In the next coach he had a counterpart among the all-white riders. I remembered the stories of World War II soldiers and how they played cards and other games of chance while aboard troop trains and ships, so I called out and inquired if anyone remembered to bring a deck of cards. We were still within the city limits of Columbus when I got several affirmative answers, and seats were hastily rearranged to facilitate card playing. My card playing experience was limited to bid whist. Almost every colored person I knew played bid whist. Poker was not my game, but I was willing to learn, so when another traveler suggested poker, we needed more players. I was psychologically ready to learn new things, and since poker was new to me, the facts were clear: No more than two of us were interested; we needed more players; somebody had to make contact next door, and since I was the one who wanted to learn, I also knew who would have to cross the platform that joined the racially segregated coaches. So I found something to keep the door ajar so that "my side" could monitor my safety, and then crossed what was my Rubicon and came face-to-face with as many white airmen as there were colored servicemen behind me.

Using the experience of playing quarterback, I assessed my situation, and in a matter of fact tone I announced, "We need two poker players." More than a hundred eyes scanned my body. No one spoke. I broke the silence and said, "Look, I want to learn how to play poker, so which two of you want to help teach me?" A few of them rose from their seats. I had to quickly determine if they were advancing toward me as friend or foe, and if it was foe, how quickly should I get my little butt to a safer place. Then I spotted a short, skinny lad who appeared to be my age, and I said: "What about you, Assless, wanna play some poker?" A smile came to his face, and he said, "Assless, by God, I been called lotta things, but never Assless." There was laughter among the riders. Someone else blurted out to the young white boy, "Assless, damn if that colored boy ain't right. Where is your ass boy?" When the roar subsided, Assless answered me. "I ain't too good at poker, but hell, it sounds like I know more 'n' you, so what the hell, let's go." Someone else shouted out, "I'll play if y'all don't play that draw crap. I play stud."

At least 12 of us went to the rear. Both doors were now propped open, and after giving up their seats to make room for card games, some of the colored airmen went forward and started another process -- colored boys and white boys getting to know each other. Assless said he'd teach me the game so that I could really learn, because, he added, "That stud playing jackass is my cousin, and I taught him to play. He don't know jack shit. Besides, he cheats."

Colored and white boys from Valdosta exchanged glances of recognition, and before long a strange new kind of segregation was taking place. White and colored players from the same city played together, reinforcing the truth that color is the least important consideration when you're among "your own kind." Even though Assless was from Florida, he and I recognized something in common that signaled "our own kind."

As our train headed toward Birmingham on that June morning the coaches seemed like rolling ovens. We opened the windows, and within 15 minutes the purpose of separating us by race was nullified. Everybody was black. Our seats were downwind from a billowing smokestack atop the coal burning engine. The filth was so immediate and permeating, that one white observer said, "Well now, I'll just pretend I'm colored." His former schoolmate jokingly told him, "The colored folks sure as hell don't want no white trash. Matter-of-fact, who does want you?"

These new relationships were moving to a new level characterized by lies, "trash talking," and revelations for leaving home. A white boy from Daytona Beach, Florida, said he just wanted to kick somebody's ass. The cops and a judge warned that if he kicked one more ass in Daytona Beach, they would shoot him in his ass. So the judge decided that if he was going to kick somebody's ass anyway, it might as well be a North Korean. We were put on a train and told when to get off, so we played cards and didn't concern ourselves with time. Time passed like the deal.

In Birmingham we increased our load of servicemen and headed for Memphis. When someone felt sleepy, he napped where he sat. Assless snored, and while he slept I became more adventurous and advanced to more of the front coaches. To my surprise, each coach was converted into a casino. Colored boys and white boys shot craps, played poker, and there was in progress one game of "Georgia skin," a game my daddy warned me not to play. He predicted. "If you start at midnight, you'll likely be broke and piss on yourself before dawn."

We were on the outskirts of Memphis when a colored marine taught me the rules of a new game called "tonk." He was the biggest winner, so I reasoned that he must know something, if only how to cheat and not get caught.

My fortune was increasing as the train stopped. About ten minutes later we started moving again. Someone noticed that the coaches carrying the Air Force recruits had been disconnected, and that those of us now riding up front would make the trip to Camp Pendleton in California along a different route. Suddenly I heard myself shout a few expletives, as I raced to the exit and leapt from

35

the slowly moving train and headed in the direction of the disjoined coaches. Fortunately, the passengers on the portion of the train that I was chasing could see my pursuit, and Ira Lee Carmichael and my new pal, Assless, rushed to the rear platform to encourage my progress. After I mustered a strong surge, they pulled me aboard. I collapsed. Less than a hundred yards further the train stopped again. It had reached the terminal -- where it was headed for a three-hour layover. I had chased a train headed for the parking lot. Ira Lee, Assless, and I looked at each other. One of them said, "What do you say at a time like this?" My reply: "Don't say anything 'cause I ain't sure if I want to laugh or cry." The three of us caught each other's eyes again and did both.

Navy Shore Patrolmen (SP's), came aboard and authorized us to disembark. My new buddy and I decided to stay together and find a place to buy a cold drink. The SP said we would have to go separate ways to find what we wanted. Assless spoke up. "We ain't gonna bother nobody. All we want is a Coke." The patrolman retorted with something about being bothered himself, particularly by what he called my buddy's smart-ass attitude. Something other than common sense made us stand our ground. The cop softened. "Now listen, if I hear any ruckus from you two little farts, I'll come on the double, kicking ass." It was a good rest. Assless and I were inseparable during the rest of the trip.

Three days later we arrived in San Antonio, Texas. Sergeants and corporals in uniforms pressed and fitted for a good impression stood along the concrete platform to greet us. Our on-board supervisor said we were to remain seated until we received another briefing.

It was a short wait before a very tall blue-eyed sergeant stood in the doorway and commanded, "When you get off this train, you'll form two columns and march over yonder to those buses. There will be no talking between the time I get through until you take your seat on a bus." He paused for effect, then continued, "Now, y'all are gonna be instructed to do a lot of things. There's three ways of doing them: the right way, the wrong way, and the Air Force way. You're gonna do everything the Air Force way, and that means you're to sound off loud and clear the answer to any question I ask, and your answer will be *yes sir* or *no sir*. Do I make myself clear?" He heard a few who said, "Yes Sir," but it seemed to lack uniformity and volume. The sergeant shouted, "I can't hear you." "Yes Sir" was better the next time. He was pleased and further instructed, "Pick up your bags and follow me." His words sounded familiar. Just then I remembered my grandfather, an African Methodist Episcopal minister, quoting the command of Jesus Christ to the fishermen: "Pick up your nets and follow me." The prospects for the fishermen were immediately better than those that awaited us.

The Sunday afternoon June Texas sun bathed us in perspiration, which streamed through three days of soot and grime. Finally, our convoy of blue buses halted in the middle of the thoroughfare near the main gate at Lackland Air Force Base. Several hundred recruits had arrived earlier and had formed rows, four deep, stretching at least three city blocks. It was an awesome sight.

Until three days ago when Assless and a few other white boys entered the colored car, I had never been part of a racially integrated group of more than a dozen folks, and then we colored participants were generally serving the whites. Now I was among a mixed assembly of more than 2,000. There was a kind of nervous gaiety in the air. Quick conversations started among strangers, each person reaching out to offer, and hoping to receive, a gesture of understanding of the common state of apprehension. Suddenly, with promoting from none and a surprise to all, a daredevil broke the calm. Everything about the youngster was different. He wore western boots, a western hat, western shirt, jeans, and a heavy shoulder strap held his guitar firmly on his back. He just couldn't resist a chance to play for the captive audience. All eyes turned forward to the position he assumed, which was not where he had been told to remain. He offered us an original western composition and was actually allowed to finish an entire verse before he was quietly circled by everyone who wore a stripe on his sleeve.

A brash little corporal, whose name tag read DUNCAN, approached the musician, extended his arms as a mother reaching for a newborn, and in a calm voice, ordered the troubadour to,

38

"Give me that guitar, and if I see you move one inch from where I tell you to stand, I'll remove these guitar strings and stick them, one-by-one, up you know where, followed by the rest of the instrument, which will be followed by my boot."

When the final convoy of buses arrived, they joined the already assembled horde that came from urban centers, townships, barrios, farms, and ghettos. We represented almost every American community. There were graduates and dropouts of high schools, colleges, and seminaries. Some of them volunteered for military serial numbers rather than being assigned a prison ID. After the masses were formed into units of approximately 70 men, it became apparent that Assless and I would be separated. So I asked Corporal Duncan for permission to say goodbye. He politely and quietly asked: "Now just tell me what you think would happen if every man here wanted to say goodbye to somebody else down yonder?"

I answered, "Then they would have to ask."

He actually smiled and said, "You've got exactly three minutes."

I left the formation and started searching, and when I spotted his little flat body, I headed through a line of men and was near my train partner when I heard the command, F-L-I-G-H-T, A-TEN-HUT." Every man in his section stiffened. I had waited too late. He caught a glimpse of my face, and we both seemed disappointed. "R-I-G-H-T FACE." They turned. "F-O-R-W-A-

39

R-D, M-A-R-C-H." They started to move. Their lines were unsteady and an unsteady airman near Assless swayed and veered a little, but a little space was all I needed to see all of him.

We had challenged some enduring Southern customs and mores. And, because of our common geography and social heritage, we also knew of relationships that transcend race, even in the ugliness of segregation. Now the Air Force would further reorder our lives. But for three days we were two special boys flaunting a kind of regional arrogance, and we enjoyed ourselves. He crossed the train door to enter a card game because he was cocky, brash, and confident. I stood there inviting integration from a potentially explosive platform because I was cocky, brash, and confident. We had passed each other's first test. In Memphis we gave reasonable notice to a SP that the system would have to accommodate our new friendship. After all, we were now "men," en route to preserve the American system, and we felt entitled to comment on how we wanted it to be.

Ironically, I don't remember if we formally exchanged real names. I called him "Assless;" he called me "Podner." Each of us responded to our greeting. We had spent our time together.

We never met again.

Hall's Arrival

The screen door to barrack 1375 opened gently, and Corporal Davis yelled "AH-TEN-HUT". We stood erect. Sergeant Wayne Hall walked into our lives. He was too tall to be short, and too short to be tall. His three stripes gave him the option to be whichever he chose. For at least two minutes he paced silently. We stood and waited, each of us knowing for certain that his first words would set the tone for basic training, and that they would be personally directed to each man, although delivered to the collective.

"Welcome to Lackland Air Force Base. I am your Flight Chief. I think basic training can be fun. It can also be a bitch. Most of you won't do anything here harder than what you've done at some point in your life. If you are not used to hard work, or keeping tight schedules, or doing more than one thing at a time, or if you're used to having somebody feed you and wipe your butt, then you've got eight hard weeks ahead of you."

That wasn't such a bad speech. I caught Albert McCloud's eyes and we nodded agreement. Then Sergeant Hall told us how we would be trained -- so many hours in the classroom testing what we already know and learning new skills and techniques to prepare us for our roles as airmen. He promised that we would march, and sometimes we would run, to take shots, for medical examinations, to the gas chamber for training, to the rifle range, to

KP duty, and for a few more shots. But he cautioned, "In order to do all these things in the allotted time, some of you might have to change your habits. There are three ways of doing things ….," His speech was interrupted by, yes, the cowboy, who himself inserted, "The wrong way, the right way, and the Air Force way." Sergeant Hall very calmly said, "Thank you private." Then he slowly walked to the subordinate and added, "If you ever interrupt me again, not even your mama will recognize your ass at your funeral." Then he continued: "A lot of you have a pretty good education, and you probably know how to do a lot of things right. He managed a slight smile and added, "If you're already doing things the Air Force way, then you're already screwed up.' It was a nice place for relief laughter. Following a few more general remarks, he pulled off his plastic pith helmet with three stripes painted to designate his rank; he wiped his brow and began our training.

Sergeant Hall started by giving us the rules of the barrack. Most of the rules were prefaced with "THERE WILL BE NO." He then told one airman to walk to the barrack door and watch for visitors. Our leader continued, loudly enough for his words to reach the sentry. "The military is built on courtesies and customs, and communicated in acronyms. R-H-I-P means rank has its privileges." And patting his chevrons, he added, "I worked hard for these three stripes, and so did every other non-commissioned officer and commissioned officer. So, whenever a noncommissioned officer, (NCO -- anybody with at least two stripes) -- enters our barrack, the first person to see the NCO should yell, BARRACK, A-TEN-HUT." Then we heard other voices. A second lieutenant had just arrived to give his welcome, but the sentry had allowed him to enter -- without announcing, BARRACK, A-TEN-HUT. Sergeant Hall and the lieutenant faced the new airman. Hall spoke. "Airman, didn't I just tell you to call the barrack to attention when a lieutenant walks in?"

"No sir, er, mister sergeant. You said a non-commissioned officer." Hall thought for a moment and remembered his own words, then continued: "But, you dip-shit, lieutenants are officers, and since they outrank non-commissioned officers, doesn't that suggest that they are entitled to the same courtesy?"

The private made a promise. "Sergeant, I'm a-gonna listen to every word you say for eight weeks. Whatever you tell me to do; I'll do it exactly as you say... 'cause I can't go back and tell that judge I screwed this up too." He then looked at the lieutenant and said, "Beg your pardon sir." Those of us who rode the train knew immediately that his hometown was Daytona Beach, Florida.

Sergeant Hall just shook his head and announced: "Let's form some lines and learn to march."

Somewhere, at this very moment, at least two GIs form that fundamental and omnipresent military symbol - a line. From the moment I arrived at Lackland Air Force Base, it seemed I was in one continuous line. There was a line to eat, a line to get fitted for clothes, and -- a truly life changing experience -- the line to use the toilet -- in a row of stools – without cubicles. Generally, lines are more efficient than random rushing for moving large numbers of persons. But civilian and military lines differ entirely in their purpose and time. Learning to march, like all military instructions, was not done for the individual's benefit and had to be presented in repetitive stages to allow for extinction of all civilian habits. We had earlier been instructed that on the command of "ATTEN-HUT" we were to stop doing whatever engaged us, to stand erect and remain motionless. Our lines were in disarray. Short and tall stood next to fat and skinny, looking like a band of wanderers who had been shocked into temporary stillness.

Hall deliberately allowed this mess to form, so that he could restructure us into a properly aligned unit. He started. "I want each of you to look to your right, and if the man next to you is shorter than you, trade places, and if the next man is also shorter than you, trade places with him. What I'm hoping we end up with is four long lines with the tallest men in front and the shortest in the back." I took one look at everybody in my line and immediately took my short frame to the last position. Only a couple of the others were as short, and they followed me. After some minor disputes over who had outgrown whom, each man had a position appropriate to his height. Sergeant Hall accepted what he saw. I didn't. From my position all I could see was the back of heads and shoulders, but it was a slight improvement from my original spot which was eye level to the ass of a much taller fellow. Still, I knew that whatever our destination, from my position I would be the last to know. But my concerns were not the purpose of this exercise.

For the next few minutes we walked up and down the street in front of the barrack. We comprised four rows. Each row was called a squad, and the tallest man at the head was called, not surprisingly, the squad leader. We had taken our first steps as a unit, but the formation needed one final alteration. Wayne Hall walked to the rear where we short airmen stood at attention. He gave us an inspection. We all waited for something to destroy our day, not because we had done anything to deserve it, but flight chiefs often chew ass when they feel like it, not necessarily when it's deserved. He asked our names. I was quick. "Alexander, James Edward, AF14417061. Sir." He was equally snappy. "Alexander, when I ask your name, just give me your last name, first name, middle initial. If every man gives me every name some mamas hang around their children's necks, we'll be here all day." He moved to the next airman and, with his mouth less than two inches from the other trainee's ear, he shouted, "Do you understand me, Alexander?" He almost scared the piss out of me, and the other airman almost fainted and yelled out his own mane ---in reverse order. It was one of those rare moments when everybody present, including Hall, decided to laugh at what was truly a funny chain of events. After that 30-second breather, Hall also told the

45

three of us that we should sue the city for building the sidewalk so close to our butts.

When he was ready, he called us shorter airmen to the front. Each, in turn, was ordered to attention directly in front of the appropriate squad leader. The chief's instructions: "Now when I say FOR-WARD-HARCH, I want you to begin the march in a straight line. The flight will follow your pace." He offered a carrot. "Now, one of you can earn the position of Right Guide. All you gotta do is show me you've got some marching potential. Whoever looks best will always march up here -- upwind from all the farts." That was enough incentive. He also offered a bonus: "If the Right Guide doesn't screw up and cause me any trouble, he will automatically make PFC at the end of basic training."

Finally, it was my turn. I wanted the job, and since I was the last to audition, the squad leaders apparently felt I was the best of a bad batch, so they offered hushed helpful hints: "Walk a little faster." "Slow down, dammit." "Veer to your left." "Alexander, inch your ass to the right."

As each of us finished our performance, we took our original places at the rear and continued marching, minus a designated marching leader. Then we heard, "FL-I-G-H-T-- HALT. Alexander, front and in the position of Flight Right Guide." I needed that. As I sped to the fore, I heard Nathaniel Baldwin say, "Well, I'll be damn; he saved his little ass again." Nathaniel knew me well. He, Benjamin Plumber, and I, had

46

walked together as friends and classmates every day of our lives from first grade in 1939, through high school, and into this same basic training flight.

Our leader said, "This is the way Flight 1607 will look every time I say fall-in." Before resuming, he offered some additional possible rewards for good performance. "Now you squad leaders and the Flight Right Guide will have to do a little extra to earn those automatic stripes. You'll have to assume duties as flight officers and take on other responsibilities that I assign. But, sometimes, when the entire flight is assigned certain duties, such as KP, you flight officers will be excused." This time Nathaniel's expletive was audible.

The sergeant continued. "Our barrack also has an extra room upstairs, and I usually let the Right Guide have it, so Alexander, move upstairs."

"Yes sir, Sergeant."

Franklin Williams didn't pretend to be quiet. He said, with emphasis, "This is getting out of hand."

Sergeant Hall hadn't finished. This also was organization day. "Next, I need two volunteers, but I'd like one of them to have at least a high school education. We need a Flight Secretary."

An airman stepped forward and said, "I'll do it sergeant." He was Airman Robert Bullock.

Another position was vacant. "Now I need a Latrine Chief to oversee the daily cleaning of the crapper, and its gotta be somebody who ain't gonna let anybody give him any crap."

Another muscular airman stepped forward and announced, "My name is Schwartz, Gerald. I'll be your Latrine Chief." Schwartz moved to the front, and confidently turned to see if anybody was stupid enough to challenge him.

Sergeant Hall announced that Flight 1607 was officially organized, and that the "flight officers" were the Right Guide, Squad Leaders, Secretary, and Latrine Chief.

We all knew our places. It was now time for chow. On command, I paced off in the direction of the dining hall, and to my first privilege of rank. After guiding the flight right up to the door, it was my choice to select the squad, and then that row followed me into the building. Therefore, I was always first to enter and first to be served. That also pleased me.

LACKLAND AIR FORCE BASE

DEPUTY COMMANDER
COL. F. BARTON

A. F. I. W.
BRIG. GEN. W. E. STEELE

GROUP COMMANDER
LT. COL. C. J. HALL

COMMANDING OFFICER
CAPT. J. ANDERSON

SQUADRON 3717   FLIGHT 1607

SAN ANTONIO, TEXAS
JULY 1951

FLIGHT CHIEF

SGT. W. HALL

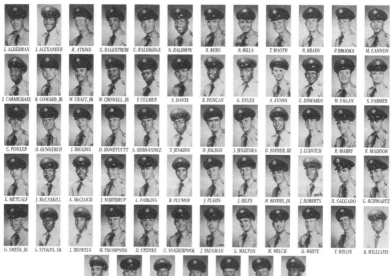

| J. ALDERMAN | J. ALEXANDER | H. ATKINS | G. BALESTRERI | C. BALDRIDGE | N. BALDWIN | R. BERG | R. BILLS | T. BOOTH | R. BRADY | P. BROOKS | M. CANNON |

| T. CARMICHAEL | B. COWARD, JR. | W. CRAFT, JR. | W. CROWELL, JR. | F. CULMER | S. DAVIS | R. DUNCAN | G. DYLES | A. EVANS | E. EDWARDS | W. FAGAN | S. FARMER |

| C. FOWLER | H. GUNNERUD | J. HIGGINS | D. HONEYCUTT | A. HERNANDEZ | T. JENKINS | D. JOLSON | J. JESZENKA | D. JOYNER, III | J. LUDVICH | R. MABRY | E. MADDON |

| E. METCALF | J. McCASKILL | A. McCLOUD | J. NORTHRUP | L. PARKINS | B. PLUMER | J. PLAIN | J. RILES | H. RIVERS, JR. | J. ROBERTS | D. SALGADO | G. SCHWARTZ |

| G. SMITH, JR. | S. STOKES, SR. | J. TROWELS | W. THOMPSON | D. UPDYKE | C. VANDERPOOL | J. VAUGHAN | G. WALTON | H. WELCH | D. WHITE | T. WILLIS | R. WILLIAMS |

| F. WILLIAMS | B. WORKIN | N. WORHTY | L. YORK | U. YORK | H. BRISON | W. WILLIAMS |

Basic Training - July 1951

SPECIAL ORDER   EXTRACT   10 August 1951
NUMBER   188

20. Having compl prescribed course for US Carbine Cal. .30 M1 fol Pvts, unless otherwise indicated, (N), unless otherwise indicated, ATRC, Flt 1607, 3717th Tng Sq, are classified as indicated. Information will be entered on DA AGO Form 20 of Amn concerned. Date fired 28 July 1951. Airmen not indicated by asterisk (*) are promoted to the temporary (AFUS) grade of Private First Class under provisions of AFR 39-30, 24 March 1950.

NAME	AFSN	CLASSIFICATION	SCORE	
ALEXANDER, JAMES E.	AF 14 417 061	Marksman	154	(N)
ALDERMAN, JAMES A.	AF 14 422 254	Unqualified	126	
ATKINS, HARRY W.	AF 14 419 993	Sharpshooter	165	
BALDRIDGE, CLARENCE T.	AF 15 456 708	Sharpshooter	162	
* BALDWIN, NATHANIEL C.	AF 14 417 043	Marksman	150	(N)
BALESTRERI, GENE R.	AF 14 411 798	Sharpshooter	160	
BERG, RONALD J.	AF 17 332 587	Marksman	144	
BILLS, RALPH E.	AF 13 386 200	Sharpshooter	156	
BOOTH, THOMAS L.	AF 14 419 995	Marksman	151	
BRADY, RICHARD A.	AF 14 419 991	Marksman	147	
BRISON, HAROLD D.	AF 19 412 277	Sharpshooter	155	
BROOKS, PAUL E.	AF 13 412 458	Marksman	146	
BULLOCK, ROBERT M. JR.	AF 13 386 205	Sharpshooter	164	
CANNON, MATTHEW E.	AF 14 422 247	Marksman	133	(N)
CARMICHAEL, IRA A.	AF 14 417 057	Marksman	131	(N)
CRAFT, WILLIAM N. JR.	AF 15 449 316	Expert	179	
COWARD, BARNWELL E. JR.	AF 14 422 253	Marksman	145	
CROWELL, WILLIAM JR.	AF 14 426 433	Marksman	152	(N)
* CULMER, FLOYD D.	AF 14 426 438	Unqualified	117	(N)
DARGAN, JAMES W.	AF 14 404 343	Marksman	138	(N)
DAVIS, SIDNEY E.	AF 15 456 704	Sharpshooter	158	
DUNCAN, REBECKER E.	AF 14 417 045	Sharpshooter	159	(N)
DYLES, GEORGE	AF 14 426 435	Marksman	144	(N)
EDWARDS, ELLSWORTH	AF 14 426 437	Unqualified	114	(N)
EVANS, ALEX G.	AF 18 399 152	Unqualified	119	
FAGAN, WALLACE R.	AF 17 328 031	Sharpshooter	176	
FARMER, SHERRILL G.	AF 15 459 566	Marksman	148	
FOWLER, CHESTER N. JR.	AF 17 332 586	Sharpshooter	167	
GUNNERUD, HAROLD D.	AF 17 332 588	Marksman	142	
HALE, BILLY G.	AF 13 386 203	Marksman	151	
HERNANDEZ, ANTONIO	AF 14 426 401	Sharpshooter	162	
HIGGINS, JACKIE R.	AF 19 416 879	Unqualified	114	
HONEYCUTT, DONALD E.	AF 14 419 989	Sharpshooter	168	
* JENKINS, THOMAS JR.	AF 14 417 058	Marksman	154	(N)
* JESZENKA, JACOB	AF 19 417 525	Marksman	147	
JOYNER, ERNEST III	AF 14 422 248	Sharpshooter	156	(N)
JULSON, DUANE M.	AF 17 332 585	Sharpshooter	158	
* LUDVICH, DONALD W. JR.	AF 25 573 685	Marksman	148	
MABRY, JAMES M.	AF 15 459 571	Marksman	136	
MADDEN, RAY	AF 15 449 314	Unqualified	122	
MARTIN, WESLEY G.	AF 17 332 593	Sharpshooter	155	
* MC CASKILL, JACK	AF 14 417 062	Unqualified	109	(N)
MC CLOUD, ALBERT	AF 14 417 046	Unqualified	115	(N)
METCALF, CARL I.	AF 19 416 878	Unqualified	122	
* METCALF, EDWARD E.	AF 19 416 883	Sharpshooter	168	
NORTHRUP, JACK T.	AF 14 419 992	Marksman	148	
PARKINS, LERAY M.	AF 19 404 030	Marksman	150	
PLAHN, JOHN C.	AF 17 328 026	Sharpshooter	171	
PLUMER, BENJAMIN F. JR.	AF 14 417 060	Unqualified	114	(N)
RILES, JIMMIE	AF 18 399 151	Marksman	152	
RIVERS, HARRY J. JR.	AF 14 411 865	Sharpshooter	163	
ROBERTS, JOHN N.	AF 14 417 056	Marksman	136	(N)
SALGADO, DANIEL E.	AF 14 426 400	Sharpshooter	156	
SCHWARTZ, GERALD	AF 15 456 700	Marksman	153	
SMITH, DANIEL L. JR.	AF 18 392 449	Sharpshooter	165	
STOKES, CLARENCE H. SR.	AF 14 426 432	Marksman	142	(N)
THOMPSON, WAYNE E.	AF 17 328 024	Sharpshooter	167	
TOBEY, CHESTER M.	AF 18 392 530	Expert	185	
* TROWELS, JOHN A.	AF 14 417 069	Sharpshooter	160	(N)
UPDYKE, DON W.	AF 15 459 572	Unqualified	127	
VANDERPOOL, CHARLES R.	AF 14 422 256	Sharpshooter	169	
VAUGHAN, JAMES T.	AF 24 264 698	Marksman	150	
WALTON, GORDON	AF 17 328 023	Unqualified	115	
WELCH, HERBERT T.	AF 14 422 252	Unqualified	126	
WHITE, DONALD D.	AF 13 412 459	Sharpshooter	158	
WILLIAMS, ROY O.	AF 14 426 406	Sharpshooter	170	(N)
WILLIAMS, FRANKLIN D.	AF 14 417 042	Marksman	137	(N)
WILLIAMS, WALTER C.	AF 14 421 931	Marksman	144	(N)
WILLIS, TED L.	AF 17 319 069	Sharpshooter	174	
WORKIN, RICHARD O.	AF 17 332 589	Marksman	146	
WORTHY, NATHANIEL	AF 14 417 044	Marksman	138	(N)
YORK, LESLIE E.	AF 18 410 433	Sharpshooter	166	
* YORK, UTAH C.	AF 18 410 422	Sharpshooter	165	

BY ORDER OF LIEUTENANT COLONEL WALL:

OFFICIAL: FRANK P. WALTHALL
                           Major   USAF
[signature: Frank P. Walthall]   Adjutant
FRANK P. WALTHALL
Major   USAF
Adjutant

James and Franklin Williams
Basic Training 1951

A Taste of Freedom

For the first two weeks of training we were restricted to the immediate area of our barrack. On the third Sunday we were ordered to dress in our best uniform and fall in. From my guide position I could see the chapel and was prepared to stop there for services. But when we passed the steeple I had no idea where were headed, and if I didn't know, everybody following me would learn the secret at the same time.

Finally, we arrived at Mitchell Hall, named in honor of General Billy Mitchell, a hero of World War II, who demonstrated the power of the airplane to sink ships. I entered through the front door into an auditorium bigger than the combined spaces of the three largest colored churches in Valdosta, my only comparison. Furthermore, there was no balcony, as there was at the movie theaters in Valdosta, where colored patrons sat. My eyes, conditioned by 17 years of racial separation, searched for a fellow Valdostan, or any colored airman. Instead, it was a white airman from another flight who sat at my side. When he said "Howdy," his Southern accent affirmed that both of us were learning new social skills.

Suddenly there was an unusual sound of drums; starting slowly and softly and ending loudly, a level which I later learned to call a crescendo. Then a white man appeared and introduced the performers. During the next 45 minutes we watched jugglers, magicians, comics and musicians. Before this day I had never seen a cello or violin, but I had seen some other instruments while standing on the curb watching the Valdosta High School band march in parades. We did not have a band at Dasher High School.

During the intermission, long lines formed for refreshments. I kept my seat. Soon, young civilian white girls served refreshments to those of us still seated. I couldn't help wondering what my grandfather would say of this day. He once predicted that colored folks would eventually move from serving to also being served, but we also had to do extra work to command our place at the front of the line.

Later that evening as I sat and shined shoes, I tried to understand how my life was changing. I had not yet learned new words like *transition* and *perspective* to help me understand the rapid shifts in thoughts and behavior. Self-teaching comes slowly, but that day I added the word *crescendo* to my expanding vocabulary. It was a good day.

Chapter Three: SWING LOW SWEET CHARIOT – I NEED A NEW RIDE

God and the Library of Congress

On a day when Flight 1607 had KP duty, and the flight officers were excused, Sergeant Hall summoned Bullock and me for a special assignment. He asked us to do a small research project at the library, requesting "Just a couple of sentences on a couple of subjects."

During the 10 minute stroll to the library, Bullock admitted that he missed his family and home, but it was his remarks about research that caught my attention. He was a white male college graduate, and he talked and acted like other educated persons in my flight, so I figured he was probably rich too, having received the kind of education good money buys. Bullock remembered late night study sessions and the amount of time spent researching his thesis. *Researching what?* Whatever that word was - thesis - it was obvious that a couple of sentences would be easy for him. On the other hand, I was simultaneously nervous and exhilarated, as memories of my last visit to a library resurfaced.

At the age of seven I walked into the library in Valdosta, and was commanded by the white librarian, "Boy, you get out of here." Shortly thereafter I, concluded that she resented me entering the front door. I returned and entered the back door, but was again ejected by the librarian and the police, because colored folks were not allowed in that "public" facility. Now I was en route to the library at Lackland, with permission to enter. This time, I had questions, the first being: where did they get all those books? But the most pressing question was: how will I find the information for Sergeant Hall? My frustration mounted as I saw Bullock dart through an aisle, apparently on a familiar course to the proper section.

My civilian teachers had warned me of this day. They had even used part of their meager paychecks to purchase training aids to help students meet the challenge. Even though every textbook I had from first grade through high school was first used by white students, using second hand books was no excuse for not using them more effectively. Now, I stood there as a high school graduate, yet unable do a simple library assignment. It was an awful feeling, and I felt that I had done my teachers a disservice, and a terrible harm to myself. I felt ashamed and started to lie.

Expecting that Bullock would soon finish, I took a book from a shelf; opened it and pretended that something else had captured my attention. Within minutes he tapped my shoulder. He was finished. I told him I had found a good book that I didn't want to leave right now. He left, leaving me in worse shape than before we left the barrack. Back there, I was unaware of my deficiency.

Here, I was face-to-face with my inadequacy and I felt uneducated and alone.

About 15 minutes later, someone stood behind me and asked, "Can I help you find something, Airman?" It was the librarian -- another white woman. By the grace of God, the line had been drawn from "Boy, you get out of here," to a gentle offer of assistance. The circle was complete.

Pride; not common sense, answered the librarian. "Oh, no ma'am, I'll find it myself." She went away. I continued to lie.

A half hour or so later she returned. "How's it going, Airman?" Exasperation softened my response. "OK, I guess." She sensed my turmoil. "What's your name, and where are you from?" "My name is Alexander, James E., and I'm from Valdosta, Georgia."

Every thought of this predicament convinces me that she hastily pasted together fragments of the social order in 1951 and concluded: Valdosta, Georgia + colored child + racial segregation = no library experience. I could feel her mind scrambling for an approach that would assuage my discomfort. It was that split second when total strangers grant to each other a measure of trust. The glint in her eyes flashed excitement. She had found a way. Looking at my bewildered face, she said: "I'm sorry I forgot to tell you about our *new* filing system. We just changed to the Library of Congress filing system, and it's probably quite different from the one you're used to. Would you like for me to show you how the

Library of Congress system works?"

That was such a neat stroke. I accepted, and she pulled a drawer from a file cabinet and walked me through my first steps, just as a mother steadies a child to walk and expand the infant's horizons. My teacher then guided me to the publication I needed. And, to guarantee that my work had a special quality for Sergeant Hall, she copied the appropriate pages. I thanked her, and as I fumbled for my fatigue cap and the doorknob, she looked at my relief and said, "Good luck to you Alexander, James E., from Valdosta, Georgia."

My guts burned and I found myself moving in a direction opposite the barrack. A couple of blocks later I reached the edge of the giant parade field and quietly selected a temporary haven near the display of vintage World War II aircraft. I sat and wept. Seventeen years of tears ran freely.

Finally, I stood and swept the ground with my brogan boots and covered the wet spots of my despair. In that gesture I symbolically recognized the pain of the past, and gave myself a clean slate to chart a new direction. And then I prayed for help; for a chariot to "swing low" and lift me out of a cavern of ignorance. My boot print also helped me to fix the spot where I vowed to return, with God's help, at another time; as another person.

Another Orientation

Almost immediately after basic training began, we received a series of orientations. The subject was always the same: We must learn to live and act as a team. Our schedule fostered mutual dependence. When the lights signaled the beginning of our new day, we hastily made our beds with the proper hospital corners, dressed, completed morning grooming, inspected each other for proper wear of the uniform, and took our positions in formation on the street. Seventy three men, 73 different personalities, from almost as many communities, had found a common purpose and forged a communal plan.

One day our training ended early. There was still enough sunlight for a stroll within a two block area. I wandered off alone. As I approached the P-T field, a large formation of new arrivals, still clad in civilian clothes, trampled their way into lines that made each man appear disconnected from the whole. Less than a month ago I had stood here and was briefed by a second lieutenant, whose use of polite language made his threats moderately credible. These young men were to be greeted by a master sergeant, the highest enlisted rank at that time.

He paced atop the platform that was used by P-T instructors to lead calisthenics. Six chevrons on his sleeves gave him the authority to proclaim that he was in charge, and everyone present knew it, including two second lieutenants who came to see how it's done. The sergeant had carefully orchestrated this performance, and years of practice made him confident. The time of day was as much a part of his plan as was his lofty position, for he stood facing the sun, so that the day's final rays would light his face and uniform. And, from that angle, he could synchronize his conclusion with the final burst of daylight, thus making sure his message would be the last significant words the trainees heard that day.

At the proper moment, according to his timetable, he spoke - without a megaphone. "Men, I'm your First Sergeant. As you learn the chain of command, you'll get to know everybody in the chain who is responsible for getting you through basic training. So, I'm your First Sergeant. Some folks have said that First Sergeants think we're second in command to God." He paused, as though waiting for the entire base to be quiet, then nonchalantly turned at the proper angle to fully expose his chevrons, and added, "We are." At that moment it was quiet enough to hear a rat piss on cotton. He continued. "I don't know, nor do I care, where ya come from, what'cha did before ya got here, or where ya go when ya leave here, but during the next eight weeks, I guaren-damn-tee ya, I'll know everything ya do, including when ya sleep, eat, and when ya crap."

He surely must have known that, at that moment, each trainee could have used the latrine. I certainly felt the urge, and I was not his target audience. But his speech had just begun. "I'm just a poor boy from Tenn-er-see who entered the 'ol Army' in 1923. I love my job very much. I love the Air Force very much. I put my uniform on a little over 28 years ago, and I'll probably die in it. I've been a First Sergeant longer than most of ya been alive." Something told me that last sentence was intended for the second lieutenants. Another pause emphasized his longevity, and he continued. "Common sense ought to tell ya I've heard damn near every lie that's been told, so don't lie to me. You'll find me a fair man, but if you give me or your flight chief one ounce of crap, you'll discover that I'm the worst son-of-bitch you'll ever meet."

For the next few minutes his remarks were essentially what any master sergeant could have said, with the power to enforce it. But this was not just any master sergeant. He was a white man from the Deep South, addressing an assembly who brought to this place a mélange of attitudes, prejudices, opinions, and persuasions. It was from him that they heard: "For some of ya, this is the first time you'll eat, sleep, work and play with a person of a different race or religion. Well, I'm here to tell ya, I don't particularly give a rat's ass how you feel about coloreds, whites, Mexicans, Jews, Catholics, or any combination thereof, so ya better get used to each other. I learned to do it." Then he exercised a very long pause, as though to allow each man a private interlude to begin thinking change. Just before dismissing the multitude his eyes swept over the humble masses, yet, seeming to fix momentarily on each person present, and he admitted, "Y'all look like ya got the makings to be good airmen. Make your folks proud of ya. We'll do our best together." He checked the sun, it too had heard enough. His stance was erect, feet spread apart and hands on hips as though giving an order to the troops -- and the sun: "Dismissed."

Every man reacted to the speech in a manner dictated by his own sense of justice, respect, or fear. The others had come together; they left in the same direction. I walked alone to my barrack.

The master sergeant's words, manner, and numbers were impressive. He started his military career in 1923, 11 years before I was born, and only five years after the end of World War I. During his lengthy career he had done battle in World War II, and he was now poised to do his duty in Korea. For 28 years he had followed the orders of his Commanders-in-Chief -- Calvin Coolidge, Herbert Hoover, and Franklin Roosevelt, while serving in racially segregated units. Finally, on July 26, 1948, his current Commander-in-Chief, President Harry Truman, signed Executive Order 9981, outlawing racial segregation in the Armed Forces of the United States. This white southerner could have gone home into retirement. Instead, his decision to remain in uniform necessitated a change of attitude about a whole host of things. He knew integration would work if the "system" wanted it to work. *He* was the system. His words also gave me hope that if I worked hard I should expect fairer competition from whites, coloreds, Mexicans, Jews, Catholics, or any combination thereof.

Those thoughts came to me as I rested --- in a private room --- in basic training. I was the Flight Right Guide. For the first time in my life I had competed against all of the above --- and won --- round 1.

Where to Go and What to Do

As we marched one morning during our sixth week of training, we saw in the distance another flight of newcomers, still dressed in civilian clothes. Their flight chief saw our approach and ordered the new arrivals to halt, so that they could see what he would soon demand of them. Seeing our audience, one squad leader said, "Let's show out." Sergeant Hall responded, "Shut up," then hesitated and softly added, "Just do it." We made him proud of us. At this stage of training the thud of the 72 pairs of boots following me had new meaning. It was a sound of harmony which signaled how men of such diversity had created a new connected entity. Marching was our manner of sharing synchronized pulses.

We came to a halt at a large green building and stood briefly at attention in the hot Texas sun. Inside, clerks and counselors awaited us to review our scores on the battery of Air Force Qualifying Tests (AFQT). My preference was to be a medic; to serve four years, after which I would use the GI Bill to fund my education to eventually become a doctor. Joe's funeral was less than two years ago. Gussie's voice and the notion that I could become a doctor were clear memories. I was now at the gate to a path in that direction.

Just before we entered the building, a second lieutenant stood in a shaded area and announced, "Those of you who want to become medical technicians follow me." Chester Fowler, a

Minnesotan, and I followed the officer inside. It was as though God whispered to the officer the words and timing to offer an escape from the heat, a bypass from the speculation, and a direct pipeline to where I wanted to go. He examined our scores and confirmed our eligibility to be medics. We would begin our careers at the Lackland hospital.

There was general excitement when we reassembled at the barrack. Our spirits were boosted by the thought of leaving basic training and joining the "real" Air Force.   All nine Valdostans huddled in my room to announce our destinations.

Most of our time during the last two weeks of training was spent insuring that we had our full allocation of clothing, completing medical and dental examinations, affirming the accuracy of personnel records to list our next of kin, and seeing that our dog tags showed blood type and religious preference. After all, some of that information might be useful, sooner than later, in Korea.

The other prominent activity during this final period of training was serving as gofers and general helpers anywhere a strong back was needed. One day I was assigned to an office to do whatever anyone with at least one stripe told me to do from 0700 to 1600 hours. Of course, I reported on time. When a major entered, I clicked my heels together and came to attention, although I didn't call the building to 'A-TTEN-HUT'. He gave me the command "at ease" and asked where I was from.

"Valdosta, Georgia, Sir," was my snappy reply.

He said, "Airman, we're both going to get tired of this attention and sir stuff, so just relax and make a pot of coffee." I did that with haste. Then, a sergeant told me to find a lawnmower and cut the grass. I did that with haste. At approximately 0915 hours, the major asked me what I would do if he released me.

I told him, "I will salute, do an about face and --- haul ass , I mean depart - - sir."

He said, "Do it." I did that with haste.

For the next six hours and 45 minutes I was free to wander about the base, to do, or not do, almost anything I wanted. Before I made a choice, it seemed a force guided me to the parade field, to the spot where I left tears a few weeks earlier. As I thought about the anguish that first drew me to that site, I reaffirmed my promise, that with the help of God and the Library of Congress, I would educate myself.

A few days later, on Friday, August 10, 1951, Sergeant Hall walked out of his room across from mine and yelled, "Flight 1607, fall in." We took our positions, by now, almost as Pavlovian subjects. Hall then reached into the pocket of his starched fatigues and withdrew a paper, and commanded, "ATTEN-HUT. The following personnel are hereby promoted to the rank of private first class (PFC)." He recited in alphabetic order. I didn't have long to wait, but it seemed forever before we heard Williams, Franklin. There also appeared on that same roster the notation (N) next to the names of all Negro airmen.

We congratulated ourselves and each other. Over the next couple of days, each man stenciled his name and rank on his duffle bag, packed and awaited traveling orders. We were preparing to go separate ways into the unknown.

Basic training was over. Eight weeks ago men who stood shoulder-to-shoulder as strangers had waded across chasms of culture, religion, ethnicity, race, and regionalism, were shaking hands and exchanging hearty farewells. For some, the parting evoked that most un-manly expression of the day, a final hug. When they thought no one was watching, a few even wiped their eyes.

I gave one traveler a special send-off. On our second day of training, Airman Hernandez greeted me: "Buenos dias, Senor Santiago Alexandro." When another man translated his greeting from Spanish to English, it was a gesture that touched me deeply, for it was the first time I heard my name in a foreign language, and delivered by a man from the tongue of his mother. So, on the day of his departure I asked another Spanish-speaking Airman to translate my words, and I saluted Hernandez and bade him farewell: "Adios, Senor Hernandez, mi amigo."

Two hours later I hoisted the duffle bag on my shoulder and walked about two miles to the headquarters 3700th Medical Group. Shortly thereafter I entered another barrack.

Approximately six men lounged on their bunks or stirred about, almost ignoring my approach.

Suddenly, all hell broke loose. A corporal said in a very loud voice, "Alexander, where the hell have you been? I've been waiting for you."

Another corporal joined him: "Yeah, Alexander, where the hell have you been?" It was a frightening start for a person who had left basic training less than four hours ago.

Finally, a third corporal approached and identified himself as Malone. Seeing that I was frozen with the duffle bag still on my shoulder, Malone said, "Alexander, these two vocal, crazy asses are Shelton and Grant. They never saw you before, but with ALEXANDER stenciled on your duffle bag, they simply couldn't resist giving you a bullshit welcome to scare the piss outta you." It worked. Malone removed my duffle bag, and I went to the latrine. When I returned, corporals Shelton and Grant had invited everybody in the barrack to the lower floor (bay), and one-by-one they shook my hand and individually welcomed me to what one of them said was: "The sickest bunch of SOBs in the Air Force, and the best barrack in the armed forces."

My new home was across the street from the parade field.

Chapter Four: COMING OF AGE IN A HURRY

Assignment to Ward 18

On Sunday I spit-shined my shoes and pressed my uniform. Every man in my barrack had been through this ritual and knew that tomorrow was my day to be assigned my first job as a medic. Some even suggested places to work, as though I had a choice.

My orders directed that I report to the Office of Surgical Services at 0700 hours Monday morning. At approximately 0645, I joined about 20 men and women with similar directives, including Chester Fowler. At 0659 hours, a second lieutenant and two sergeants greeted us.

In 1951 the hospital at Lackland was a wooden structure comprising three long corridors, which we called ramps that numbered A, B, and C, each stretching approximately one-half mile. Off of Ramps A and B were entrances to surgical wards, surgery, the mess hall and specialty clinics; each identified by a rectangular sign over the door.

Our assembly followed the officer along Ramp A. As we approached WARD 18, a big muscular colored staff sergeant waited in the door. His name tag read ROBINSON. He was the Ward Master, a title which recognized his proficiency as a medical technician, supervisor, trainer, and liaison between his subordinate medical attendants, doctors,   nurses, and patients. He had been informed that help was coming. The lieutenant barked: Alexander, ward 18.

Ward 18 had 47 beds lined on each side of an aisle. Each patient had his own bedside stand for small personal belongings. Because the building was not air conditioned, an electric fan rested on each stand to rearrange the hot Texas air. In the middle of the ward a side door led to a screened porch. In addition, the front portion of the ward had been compartmentalized into a bathroom, kitchen, linen closet, utility room, nurses' office, a treatment room, and two private rooms for patients with special problems.

Coincidentally, I arrived when most of the surgeons and senior nurses assembled to discuss each patient's diagnosis, surgical procedure and post-operative prognosis. Sergeant Robinson escorted me into their midst and interrupted: "Ladies and gentlemen, this is PFC Alexander, James E."

The leader of the group offered, "Welcome to the family, Private Alexander." His name tag read GOLD, and he had eagles on his collar. He was Dr. (Colonel) David Gold, Chief of Surgery.

I was assigned to the day shift, 0700-1500, the busiest period for learning and applying new skills. In quick order, Sergeant Robinson, the nurses and doctors introduced me to a vigorous on-the-job-training (OJT) regime of fundamentals. They enjoyed teaching, and I enjoyed learning. All of the nurses and doctors were white. We all sensed something new; both teachers and student were in a new learning environment. One day a doctor invited me to follow him to the surgery suite. He told me to take a seat in the corner and simply observe. A couple of hours later, as we walked back to the ward, the surgeon, a graduate of Rice University, made some comments; the most significant being: "Alexander, it takes a lot of hard work to do what you just observed. There's something about you that tells me you can do it" He, like Mister Rich, the liquor store owner in Valdosta, was offering advice and encouragement. I also heard another voice; that of my grandfather, who told me: "When you set a good course, successful people will take notice and will offer their support. That's how success breeds success."

About three months later Sergeant Robinson told me to stay after work. We made our way to the back, less-traveled corridor of the hospital so that he could instruct me with fewer distractions. He reported that my appearance and quickness to learn and apply basic medical procedures was closely observed and applauded by the doctors and nurses. That pleased him, since it also projected his teaching skills. Then he offered his counsel, not as a supervisor, but as an older colored brother preparing a 17-year-old kid from Georgia for a role in a society with strict rules for governing wide diversity of cultures, races, genders, and attitudes. Most of his military service to date was under the "old school rules" of racial segregation and early integration. He and the other colored NCOs had paved a path that he hoped I would take and make even smoother for my own advancement and for other coloreds. As we approached the end of the corridor I saw three other colored sergeants waiting to greet us. Sergeant Robinson didn't introduce me, he simply said, "Here he is." It was Master Sergeant Perry who spoke for the others. "Alexander, you're off to a good start; keep your nose clean, and we'll take care of you."

Shortly thereafter, Sergeant Robinson smiled and handed me a flyer that asked for volunteers to help the Red Cross escort patients to stock car races, football games, symphonies, rodeos and other events, both on-base and in San Antonio. Two days later I was among the medical corpsmen and Red Cross staff who escorted approximately two dozen patients to a concert performed by the San Antonio Symphony Orchestra. I was the only colored medic, and because I was escorting military patients, I was not segregated by race, as were other colored patrons at public events. Sergeant Robinson had subtly executed a bypass around another demeaning social barrier and introduced a boy from Valdosta to a new world of comfort.

Most of the patients were ambulatory, some just spending the last few days before being discharged for medical conditions and sent to VA hospitals near their families. Their conversations exuded confidence and they spoke of building futures for themselves and the nation. Their bodies were broken, but none complained.

One evening as we travelled aboard the huge ambulance to a performance of Giuseppe Verdi's opera, *Aida,* a female patient let me use something which she rightly anticipated would enhance my appreciation of that art form. On the ride home I wrote the word *libretto* in my pocket notebook.

The Blind Leading the Blind: Two Navigators

There had never been a time in my life when I had shared a meal at the same table with a white man. Dining with friends and associates is often a social event, and I was emerging from a social system where coloreds and whites, "us and them," were channeled along different social paths by omnipresent "colored" and "whites only" signs. Basic training had changed that, but in that setting each man fed himself. Now, I literally held in my hands the awesome power to decide what and in what manner a white man would receive his basic nourishment.

Almost every day in 1951 giant medical air evacuation planes landed at Kelly Air Force base near San Antonio, Texas. They were bringing wounded warriors from the Korean skies and battlefields to the hospital at Lackland Air Force Base, located adjacent to Kelly. One day on Ward 18 we greeted a jet pilot whose face was hidden behind thick bandages. His eyes had been severely damaged in an aerial dogfight and he was spending his days in darkness. My assignment, as a medical corpsman, was to see and do for him some things he hoped to someday resume doing.

Entering his room, I offered, "Good morning, Lieutenant. Welcome home."

He immediately asked, "What's your name, and are you a doctor, officer, sergeant, or civilian?"

My answer was quick and impolite: "I'm none of the above, sir I'm a PFC, so I work for a living."

His laughter was so loud that the nurse rushed to his door. It was good to see him in high spirits. When I finally introduced myself as PFC Alexander, James Edward, he asked what name I preferred: Alex, James, Jim, PFC Alexander, or "smart ass?"

I told him I preferred James Edward Alexander; and that at least once per day, it would be nice to hear him pronounce it properly.

He responded that he would call me Alex and added, "If you don't like what I call you, just make funny faces at me; since I can't see you, I won't have to ignore you." He laughed some more.

Shortly thereafter I delivered the first meal to my special patient, very much sensitive to and appreciating that my distance from Valdosta, Georgia, could be measured in miles; but there was no way to measure the nuances of the social transition taking place. This person, whose education and training qualified him to pilot a highly technical jet aircraft, was now vulnerable to and relying on the goodness of a stranger. We had traveled along separate passages to the same fork in the road. Fate dictated that we now jointly navigate our new path, but only one traveler, a seventeen year old colored boy from Georgia, could see where to steer.

Eating is a very personal function that is influenced by a seemingly endless list of options, including one's selection of seasoning, temperature, shapes, sizes, colors, textures, quantities; whether liquid or solid, raw or cooked, meatless or carnivorous. Other variables to consider are when and where one eats, and whether one eats alone.

As I observed the variety of edibles on the patient's tray, I asked, "Do you want me to feed you? Or should I identify your food choices and guide your hand to your plate? Or should I cut your food and fill your fork or spoon, so that you can feed yourself?" I simply could not resist adding, "Remember, Lieutenant, if you don't pronounce my name properly, all you'll get will be bread and water."

His answer was acceptable: "James Edward Alexander, you're a disgusting person who was probably run out of your home town." I interrupted him. "OK, sir, I'll feed you." Before we proceeded, he said, "Alex, when we're in this room together, please call me Bill." Then he opened his mouth and I offered Bill the first bite.

A few days later Bill wanted to hear his girlfriend's voice, so he held my arm, and I guided him to the telephone booth at the Red Cross lounge. Two weeks later, just before the noon meal, she came to visit. She offered to feed him, but he declined, jokingly telling her that PFC James Edward Alexander needed the practice. It was an acceptable excuse for her, while masking his real purpose. He and I had refined our dining signals: his rate of chewing; the intervals between helpings based on texture; the amount of sugar, cream, or lemon he liked in his beverage; and when and how to wipe the crumbs from his face without disturbing his bandages. I was there to properly feed his body, thus giving him the energy to appreciate her presence. She was there to feed his emotions.

Each morning as I entered the ward and greeted the nurses and other corpsmen, Bill heard my voice and would acknowledge my arrival by asking, "Is that you Alex?" One day he asked me to read to him portions of the *San Antonio Light*, the daily newspaper. In the middle of one article he stopped me and offered this observation and a unique gift: "Alex, I have been observing your manner; and I'll bet that you will one day be a well-educated man. Let me help you get started. It will help me stay alert, and it will help you prepare for college."

His bandages hid from his view the tears that welled in my eyes as I remembered the awful experience during basic training less than three months earlier when, because of my lack of scholarship, I could not complete a simple library assignment. On that day I had knelt in agony and vowed to educate myself. On this day I announced, "Bill, you're repeating the expectations of my grandfather, and you're offering to help me keep a promise to myself. I would appreciate your help." He then asked me to resume reading, but warned that he would stop me when I mispronounced anything and promised to define for me unfamiliar words.

On another day as we visited the Red Cross lounge, we also shopped at the nearby PX, where I purchased a small pocket dictionary. Bill also bought for me a small notebook and a fountain pen. When I arrived for duty the next day, he had memorized a list of subjects that he thought I should know.

He started alphabetically. *Antigone.* I told him to spell his name. He said, "*Her* name is spelled A-N-T-I-G-O-N-E," then added, "That will naturally lead you to know something about her father *Oedipus,* spelled O-E-D-I-P-U-S, which will introduce you to Greek mythology."

My initial pronunciations of Antigone and Oedipus were "anti-gone" and "o-e-dip-ass" We laughed some more and extended the list to include both real history and mythology; the names of famous personalities, living and dead; important dates in history; and a long list of literary classics and music composers.

When we weren't learning new things, we were sharing our own histories. In high school he studied chemistry and biology and performed experiments in laboratories. He practiced basketball in a gymnasium and occasionally played in the school's marching band. There was no question that he would go to college, and so he did. Within three months after graduating from college he was enrolled in the Air Force Flight Training Program. He heard that my segregated schools did not have a science lab, gymnasium, or marching band; so I studied chemistry and biology in the same classroom, and read about experiments in used books from the white high school. Then, since our family resources were inadequate for me to attend college, twenty-one days after my high school graduation I also entered the Air Force. Our separate roads brought us to this day.

We continued our feeding, reading, and learning rituals. After a couple of months the doctors removed his bandages but shielded his eyes with specially fitted cups that allowed only a trace of light to enter his visual field. Shortly thereafter the doctors informed Bill that he was to be transferred to a VA hospital near his hometown.

Hello is the prelude to goodbye. Between our greeting and the imminent farewell we had exchanged friendship, knowledge, respect, and most profoundly, trust - that sense of mutual faith and confidence. The morning of his departure he wanted to wear his uniform rather than pajamas and robe. We did not talk much as I helped him dress. When he asked, "Alex, how do I look?" I imitated my basic training flight chief/drill sergeant and said, "I can't hear you." He knew the drill and answered, "James Edward Alexander, you reprobate from Valdosta, Georgia, how do I look?" I gave my approval and walked him to another ambulance for a ride back to Kelly AFB.

We had said hello three months ago; and as we said goodbye, he asked for my hand and said, "Thank you, James Edward Alexander. I hope to see you one of these days." I replied, "If you do sir, I'll salute you again." And I withdrew my right hand from his, saluted, and added, "Just as I'm doing now."

Later that day I took a walk to another place on the base: to a special spot on the parade field.

Seeking One's Color and One's Kind

My grandfather told me that the characteristic that most attracts humans to each other is not gender, race, ethnicity, nationality or religion; it is the quality of the mind. The medical corps was the most educated squadron on the base, so I was surrounded by persons who spoke and acted differently from anything I had heard or seen. Among the enlisted medical personnel were more pharmacists, physical therapists, biologists, and clinical psychologists than could be assembled in many civilian hospitals. Another special group of enlisted persons were male nurses, who were not yet offered commissions as officers. Most of these enlisted professionals volunteered their skills to the war effort for four years, after which they simply wanted to return to their civilian practices.

Included in this large pool of college-educated enlisted persons were many colored airmen, including Ignatius Collier, a native of New Orleans. His nickname was "Iggy", and his daily ritual was to count the number of days before he would return home and marry his sweetheart, Elsie. He also was a graduate of Xavier University School of Pharmacy, which trained many of the colored pharmacists of that time

In 1951 most Americans were born, lived, died and were buried in racially segregated communities. On base, the military structure, by necessity, demanded intermingling based on job assignment and rank. Beyond the gates, however, both military and civilians sought their own color and their own kind. As we explored the city of San Antonio, colored airmen, even in uniform, were expected to take back seats on city buses and to obey the Jim Crow laws that denied to us the liberties we were sworn to protect. The contradiction was obvious, but such awareness is a logical conclusion. Racism ignores logic and festers where ignorance takes refuge.

Another friend was Millard McNeal, a native of San Antonio, who also took basic training at the same time in another flight, and likewise chose to be a medic. When Millard invited me to meet his family it was as though I was fast forwarded into an economic and social scene that colored folks back home used to talk about as "having arrived." The McNeal's were at the crest of the city's colored society. Their home was nicely furnished, including television and electric appliances that I had only seen in Sears-Roebuck catalogs and a couple of white folks' homes in Valdosta. They took one look at a child so far from his home and immediately welcomed me into their family and included me in their social agenda. The children, Mildred, Althea, Isabelle, and Millard, called their parents Mom and Dad, and both Mom and Dad liked it when I addressed them in that manner. There was no mention of additional children. One Sunday they invited me to church and witnessed my confusion. Upon arrival they were greeted by a white man wearing a long black robe. They called him father. Then, two white women wearing long black dresses with beautifully starched white bibs approached, and they greeted them as sisters. The McNeal's were Catholics. I didn't know any Catholics in Valdosta, colored or white. Shortly thereafter, they introduced me to another social level with an invitation to something they called a debutante ball, like one of those big fancy parties they pictured in *Jet* and *Ebony* magazines.

When I was not with the McNeal's I was frequently with other young GIs, behaving as young GIs always do: work hard, and at the first moment of freedom, flock to places of entertainment, especially those places where girls congregate. Most of the colored airmen sought entertainment at a string of clubs on East Commerce Street in San Antonio.

As always, we had to pay to play, and payday was once monthly on the first day. That pay schedule frustrated even the most fiscally disciplined airmen, who often needed a loan to meet urgent mid-month expenses. To accommodate the masses, Lindbergh Keyes, a young enterprising colored airman from Washington, DC, became the alternate "finance clerk," lending money at 50% interest rate. Sure it was usurious, but his customers were all colors, genders and ranks. Furthermore, he had a built in enforcement system. If a borrower's repayment was late, Keys simply announced that he didn't have enough funds to loan and named the delinquent. Immediately, everybody forcefully encouraged the debtor to pay Keyes, even if it meant borrowing from another higher interest source. Therefore, each Keyes borrower also became a surrogate collector.

With borrowed money in our pockets we sometimes gathered at a popular joint that offered a Saturday "Matana" featuring live music. We excused the owner for misspelling *matinee*, and just flocked where another group of single women congregated.

One night in 1952 we received an unusual offer. An airman rushed into the barrack and offered to sell his 1941 Plymouth for $400. He accepted for down payment any amount the buyer could deposit -- in mid-month. Seven of us hastily collected less than $50. My contribution was $1.75. We didn't inspect the vehicle, reasoning that since he drove it to us, we could drive it to where we wanted to go.

Our first collective outing was to Ciudad Acuna, Mexico, where we frolicked until the early morning hours, leaving just enough time to drive 150 miles back in time for duty. At the border the customs official asked the routine questions: citizenship, place of birth, and things which were on the tip of our tongues to affirm that we were merely returning home. One airman, Fremont Williams, decided to do what he always did -- something outrageous and unpredictable. When the officer asked if we were bringing anything back, Fremont signaled that he had a girl. The officer ordered us to open the trunk. When the door opened it seemed that half a medical warehouse had been carefully concealed – by the previous owner. We were then questioned about stealing government property and selling it in Mexico. Suddenly the agent heard bottles, and upon closer inspection discovered the contents to be Phenobarbital, a drug that required a prescription, and no doctor would prescribe the amount he found. The agent called the FBI.

As we stood surrounded by federal agents, they asked some reasonable questions: "Who owns the car?" In unison, "We do." "Where is the registration?" In unison, "In the glove compartment – we think."

One agent suggested that we be locked up until further investigation. That's when Ignatius Collier, "Iggy," asserted himself. Iggy informed the agent that he was a registered pharmacist who wouldn't risk his license if he knew the contents of the bottles. Things were getting tense and all of us, except Fremont, were getting uncomfortable. Then an agent looked at me and asked my name.

"My name is PFC James Edward Alexander, sir, and who are you?"

He said, "I'm the guy who can send you to jail."

I responded, "I have never spent a night in jail, and I don't intend to for something I didn't do."

He looked at me and said, "I'm beginning to think you guys are telling the truth; you're too stupid to be criminals." He then grabbed my arm and led me to our car and sat me in the driver's seat, and then motioned the others to get in, as he instructed me: "Listen you little fart, you drive this car straight back to Lackland." Then he promised that we could expect a visit by the FBI tomorrow. They kept the supplies and sent us on our way. Fortunately, he didn't ask me to provide a driver's license. I didn't have one.

A few nights later I announced that I needed the car for a personal outing, even though I was still an unlicensed driver. But a license is a prerequisite that competed with the rush of hormones that often cloud the judgment of teenage males. I drove to the home of Dora, a girl I met earlier at another joint. I got there before her boyfriend Jesse, and persuaded her that an evening with me would be superior to anything she had experienced with him. Even though she mentioned that Jesse was extremely jealous, I continued the drive to a popular club in San Antonio. After all, she was talking to a self assured, newly promoted to corporal, 17 year old dude from Valdosta, Georgia; a combination too tough for the Jesse's of the world.

We sat in a booth dark enough for me to reaffirm my magic. I was in rare form, when she suddenly issued an alert: "Here comes Jesse, and he usually carries a gun." My magic turned to mush. Instinctively, I shifted to the role of quarterback and guided both of us to a huddle – on the floor. Jesse approached the area of our booth that appeared empty, but, even though he couldn't identify me, if he had lingered in the vicinity for a moment he would have heard my heart. When he passed I gave her the car keys and whispered for her to walk quietly, but hurriedly, to the car. I figured that she would make it unnoticed, but if he did observe her escape, they would have some preliminary discussion; long enough for me to find the back door --- my quarterback option. Both of us reached the automobile safely, and I drove slowly from the parking lot so as not to draw attention to a tense departure. However, I sensed that every car behind me was Jesse's. As I approached an intersection in the heart of the city two more potential hazards greeted me: the traffic light was red, and a fire truck, two blocks away, was heading in our direction. There were no other vehicles in sight, so I decided that if Jesse was following me, he should stop at the light and for the fire truck. I ran the red light. Within a few minutes, much fewer than it would ordinarily take to cover the same distance, I parked, very briefly, at Dora's door. I only hope she heard me say goodbye as I sped away.

Both incidents happened in March 1952. The FBI never contacted us. I never again contacted Dora.

Five months later I reported to work and was informed that my mentor was gone. Sergeant Robinson died on August 4, 1952, in a head-on collision of two Greyhound buses near Waco, Texas.

An Elder among Us

In a military hospital everyone understood that there would be military rules. The first directive of the day for ambulatory patients was to rise at 0630. Within 45 minutes they were expected to make their beds (with hospital corners, of course) tidy their bedside area, do personal hygiene, and walk to the mess hall for breakfast. Those patients whose conditions prevented that routine, or those who needed more attention deserved and received special treatment from the medical staff and other patients.

Most of the patients on this adult male ward were either recuperating from recent surgery or they were awaiting their turn to remove or repair hernias, varicose veins or pilonidal cysts. A few had just returned from Korea and had undergone plastic surgery to remake portions of their body that had been damaged in combat. Some were older retirees recovering from surgeries related to military service, or just repairing parts of bodies that still had some use but needed mending. One day we welcomed an elderly adult dependent. Here, you will know him as Mr. Snow.

He arrived in a civilian ambulance and entered through the rear door. Mister Snow looked older than his 85 years, and he was afflicted with a plethora of ailments incidental to old age. None of us was surprised when he announced that he had come to the hospital to die. We reassigned patients to beds to make room for him near the nurse's office. Within a couple of hours something unusual was happening that attracted everybody's attention. Three young GIs had taken seats at Mr. Snow's bedside, and each took turns wiping the newcomer's brow with a cool moist cloth. Throughout the day other privates, corporals and sergeants volunteered as mother hens for a stranger whose age and dignified presence encouraged their compassion.

After a few weeks of this attention and medications Mr. Snow's strength and vigor were noticeably improved. The real test of his recovery was not some medical examination. A more precise gauge of his improvement was his understanding and appreciation of the almost endless jokes shared among the patients. One doctor observed, "If my patients are laughing and joking, they're not crying." At first Mr. Snow only listened, but GIs tell jokes unlike any other group, so proximity simply drew Mr. Snow into the amusement circle. There is an unspoken rule that if you enjoy hearing a joke, you're invited to tell one. Some jokes, like fine wines, actually improve with age, especially when some facts are slightly altered for contemporary understanding. One day Mr. Snow joined the narrators with a tale about a cowboy and a sharecropper. Naturally, it also involved a woman, a horse and bad weather. The woman and horse were the only two characters whose honor escaped perdition and damnation. When the roar of laughter subsided, one nurse urged an encore as she recorded his tale on her note pad. She then gave him a hug and called him a very charming, very old, dirty old man. He was now a member of the club.

One day Mr. Snow wanted to teach younger men a lesson. Age and illness had not extinguished his sense of timing and drama. At an appropriate time he raised his voice and summoned me. "Private Alexander, can I have a word with you." All eyes followed me to his bedside. He sat up and asked a question. "Young fellow, when is the last time you got laid?" There was a strange silence as all eyes and ears awaited my response. I hesitated, unsure how to respond to this public inquiry. Finally, I told him the question was too personal. He quickly responded, "Ah, ha, that's the point." This was his forum so he continued. "Even if you won't tell me the last time you had a woman, do you remember her name?" Then, to avoid another long silence, he continued. "Alexander, you ought to remember the name and face of every woman who shares your bed." He then readjusted his pillow and resumed his nap. The eldest patient had just written a prescription for male maturity.

A month later the doctor told Mr. Snow that St. Peter had gone AWOL from his post at the Pearly Gates, and since God didn't allow trespassers in Heaven, he would just have to go home and live longer.

The old man insisted on three conditions of departure: 1. Rather than pajamas and robe, he would wear his best suit. 2. He would not return home in an ambulance. 3. He would walk, unassisted, out the back door where he expected his son to be waiting with the car door open.

On the eve of his discharge his son brought his clothes and shoes. We fashioned a special overnight rack in the linen closet for his wardrobe. Although every other patient denied it, someone had taken Mr. Snow's shoes and returned them under the elder's bed – after giving them a perfect spit shine. He was scheduled to leave between 1130 and 1300 hours – chow time. Almost every other patient and staff missed lunch that day. We all applauded Mr. Snow's recovery, but we also knew his departure would leave a void that we would prefer to defer. Two sergeants helped the frail gentleman tie his shoes and tie and sat with him in a scene that resembled three travelers waiting at a bus stop. Shortly before noon we heard, "Sir, your ride is here." It came from a sentry whose voice resonated disappointment. The elderly man rose and made a brief panoramic final inspection of the ward and the assembly, then braced his back and began his slow walk to the door. There was no prearranged understanding among the other patients, so the spontaneous ceremony that followed was even more touching. Each patient stood at parade rest in front of his own bed, and as Mr. Snow passed, each man snapped to attention and gave the old man a sharp salute. When he reached the rear entrance, he turned, harnessed his remaining strength, stood at attention and returned the salutes.

That afternoon there seemed little interest in playing cribbage or pinochle, but we used a lot of Kleenex that day.

Paying the Price --- and Receiving a Bonus

Sergeant Robinson had told me to learn the rules and nuances of the military. He promised that such information would help me chart my course. He also advised that I learn who has the authority to enforce the rules. Furthermore, he told me that, regardless of how policy is mandated by civilian control or how it is passed from the Pentagon to senior officers, the rules that noncommissioned officers fashion and enforce among themselves more often determine the success or failure of the military mission. In the early 1950s, all sergeants, especially master sergeants, exercised more direct control of the daily lives of the troops than all others. They performed their duties through a series of direct orders and exchange of favors. If a NCO owed you a favor, you had an account receivable that you could count on. If you owed a NCO a favor; you paid up before your discharge.

Shortly after Sergeant Robinson's death, Master Sergeant Billy Johnson ordered me to report to his office. He was the supervisor of almost all enlisted personnel who served in clinics, the pharmacy, surgery, wards, and medical supply units. I had earlier heard a full colonel instruct a major and a captain not to do something "…until you check with Billy." I had no idea why Sergeant Johnson wanted to see me, but, of course, I reported on time. He got right to the point. "Alexander, the neurosurgery wards need a good 11-7 shift corpsman. I owe the ward master a favor. You're my payment."

Everything I had learned about medicine was immediately applied while taking care of patients with brain injuries, paraplegics and other debilitating neurological disorders. In the end what they taught me was as valuable as the care I gave them. They showed me that doctor-ordered surgeries and medications work best when augmented by strong doses of one's patience and persistence. But it was the schooling I received in the early morning hours that kept me focused on a promise.

Another corpsman and I quickly developed comfortable routines to care for our patients and to have some time to ourselves to sit and relax. One morning the nurse finished reading a book and offered it to me. Many of the words, in English, seemed foreign to me. The next day I returned to the base library and checked out textbooks to begin the process of self improvement that I promised that awful day on the parade field.

In the early hours of the next morning I opened a textbook to begin to learn English grammar. My studying also excited the nurse, who offered to help me review the basics of English, reading comprehension, geography, and math. She had taught nursing before entering the Air Force, so guiding students was another skill that she extended to me. She and I even coordinated our schedules so that we would work the same five nights per week. Our sessions lasted almost a year.

Two nights before her discharge the nurse came to the ward to say goodbye. We sat and recalled how much both of us had grown together. Then, even though she was an officer, she spoke like a NCO and reminded me that I owed her a favor --- and the payment was for me to continue my studies. On her way out the door she turned and said, "It wouldn't surprise me if I read about you one day."

It Takes Time to Extinguish Bigotry

On March 17, 1953, Dave and I met on our way to chow. He wore a green patch on his lapel, and he asked me why I didn't display the color green anywhere on my white uniform: "Alexander, where is your green?"

I asked: "Dave, what are you talking about?"

He answered, "Today is St. Patrick's Day."

There were no celebrations of St. Patrick in my Valdosta community. There wasn't even a St. Patrick's church in the city, for colored or white parishioners. So I simply asked, "OK, so what?"

That gave Dave a chance to declare himself a self-appointed missionary to enlighten a heathen. "Alexander, don't you know anything? Everybody wears green on St. Patrick's Day, especially Irish-Americans like me."

Then I asked, "Why do you claim to be both Irish and American?"

He had a ready answer "My parents came to this country from Ireland, and then later became American citizens, so that makes me an Irish-American." Even though he was not the immigrant, he proudly linked himself to the nationality of his ancestors.

Even in 1953, that prompted me to declare, "Well, since my ancestors were brought here from Africa, I guess that makes me an African-American." Dave reacted swiftly and almost angrily: "What! Why do you call yourself an African-American? Are you some sort of militant?"

Approximately two months later, I donned a new suit. When I put on my brown suede shoes and stood before the mirror in the latrine, I was acceptable to attend the party in downtown San Antonio. As I exited the barrack I met Carl, another white airman who was so impressed with my appearance that he asked a familiar question: "Alexander, where are you preaching?"

Neither Dave nor Carl considered their comments racial slurs. Each man simply reflected the attitudes and expressions they brought from their civilian communities. Dave was white, so he felt free to define himself by whatever standard confirmed his perception of his human and social superiority. For me to claim the same prerogative was a challenge to his order. Carl expected that any colored man wearing a suit must be a preacher, because colored men had no business that required wearing a suit, especially on a day other than Sunday.

It takes time to extinguish bigotry, especially when the notion of inferiority springs from official pronouncements, as from the sentiments of Roger B. Taney, Chief Justice of The United State Supreme Court. He viewed all slaves and their descendants as, "Beings of an inferior order, and altogether unfit to associate with the white race, either in social or political relations, and so far inferior that they had no rights which the white man was bound to respect." [Dred Scott v. Sanford, 60 U.S. 393 (1856)]

Even some whites who thought of themselves as being without racial prejudice either initiated or participated in a most subtle form of racism. GIs tell jokes, and whenever a white jokester prefaced his offering with "Hey Alexander, you've got a good sense of humor; listen to this," what followed was an offering that poked fun at me personally or all colored folks. And the jokester's delivery was often in an unrefined, crude dialect he attributed to all coloreds. Furthermore, the preface intended to nullify my criticism, and, because he had declared me "of good humor," I also was expected to laugh at myself.

Yes, it takes time to extinguish bigotry, but any time spent liberating oneself from the yoke of ignorance and insensitivity is time well spent.

Draft Choice

There were a lot of reasons for a squadron commander to visit an airman at his duty station. In 1953, Lieutenant Robert Holmes was my Squadron Commander. Before that he was a standout player at Texas A & M. When he came to my ward, he promptly stated his purpose:

"Alexander, my research tells me you were a pretty good quarterback in high school. I'm also the squadron football coach. Come and let me see how good you are." Later that day I reported for practice, and Coach Holmes pointed to the giant parade field and said, "Y'all Give me five laps." Within a week the number of laps increased. Three observations were significant: The players were much bigger and faster than anybody I had ever faced; most of them were white; and the equipment was new. In high school our uniforms were so threadbare, that we were dubbed "The Dasher High Tigers - the ragged 11."

Four teams of approximately 25 men each formed the 6-man inter-squadron tackle football league. The rosters of each team included players who had earned letters at major universities. They taught me conditioning and playing techniques that challenged my body and mind. They also thought I was good enough to be their starting quarterback.

(Ironically, as much as I enjoyed playing football, I never read accounts of how we became co-champions. In preparation for

this book, I requested some pictures from the Historical Archives
at Lackland AFB. An alert clerk researched my name and provided
articles and statistics which I had never read.)

A Boy at the Altar – Then What?

On a hot day in July 1953, I was on leave and spending time with my mother in her kitchen in Valdosta. We were looking out the window just as a young woman stepped from the city bus. I remarked, "Kate seems to be getting younger and even more attractive." Catherine answered, "Kate and her sister are attractive. That's her sister, Julia."

Both women, natives of Abbeville, Alabama, were boarding with my long-time neighbor. Fifteen minutes later I decided to pay my neighbor a visit—and met a wife.

After polite introductions and brief conversation I somehow worked myself into an invitation to share a glass of iced tea in the shade of oak trees, a setting which naturally encourages an invitation for dinner. Even at age 24, Julia looked as young as my age 19. She also was what every teenage boy thinks about: a pretty girl who gives you attention, and she permitted me to call her Judy.

The next evening Charles Hudson, my cousin, high school classmate and a Marine also on leave joined us for dinner. We ate at 7 p.m. It was a lovely meal. I ate too much, and at 11 p.m., Charles drove me to the hospital at Moody Air Force Base to seek relief from a severely upset stomach.

Two days after my leave ended, her first letter followed me to Lackland. Every day thereafter the mailman called my name. In

December 1953, I returned home. Judy and I gave each other a belated Christmas present on December 31 – our mutual vows of marriage, uniting our destinies in directions where immediate questions outstretched our answers

On the long train ride back to Texas I reviewed my original plan to leave the Air Force at age 21 and enter college, ultimately to become a doctor. Those plans did not figure how a wife would change my life. One often lacks that kind of mature judgment at age 19, and I had not asked more experienced persons about marriage and a family. Some of the most pressing concerns were: Where will we live when she comes to Texas? If I leave the Air Force in 18 months, where will we live, if not back in Valdosta? Will I go to college, and how will I supplement my GI bill to support us?

Two months later Judy arrived in San Antonio; both of us as excited as on our wedding day. We seemed so close that it was unthinkable that we couldn't do anything we wanted. We didn't have much money, but we had each other, and we felt comfortable.

As a corporal I was ineligible for housing on the base, so we were lucky to find an apartment near the McNeal's in San Antonio. We didn't have a car, but the city bus and married GIs with transportation got me to work on time. We didn't even have a TV, but neighbors invited us to watch *The Jackie Gleason Show*, and to hear Snooky Lanson, Dorothy Collins, Russell Arms, and Gisele MacKenzie on *Your Hit Parade*.

Judy and I were products of small towns, so we behaved as tourists, visiting as much as we could afford in massive San Antonio. Furthermore, because of her heritage as a colored woman from a small Southern town, she knew how to stretch two potatoes and a pound of hamburger meat into a feast.

In April 1954, four months after our wedding day, Judy announced that we would be parents in January 1955. We sat quietly for a moment, then shouted and hugged. Then we started to wonder if our child would be a boy or girl, and with what family features, those resembling Judy or me. Finally we understood that such speculation was silly, and we prayed for a healthy child. Our excitement promoted an affectionate daily ritual. Immediately upon entering the house from work, we measured her stomach --- beginning a week after her announcement. We very quickly purchased maternity dresses, cloth diapers, clothing for either gender, and a longer measuring tape.

Shortly after the end of the 1954 football season, another officer visited my ward and also invited me to join him for a stroll. He promptly identified himself as a scout for the University of Washington, and was matter of fact about his purpose:

"Alexander, I've watched you play quarterback and halfback, and you're pretty good. In fact, you're good enough for me to offer you a chance at a scholarship at the U of W." Of all the subjects we might have discussed, a football scholarship was not what I imagined. He also knew it was a surprise, so he awaited my response and monitored my reactions. I simply walked and wondered if I was dreaming.

He broke the silence. "Because of your size, you will be competing against bigger and taller boys, but you have two attractive attributes: As a quarterback in practice, you will make any offense better, and you will make any defense more alert. And you're one fine passing halfback with a rifle for an arm. Those skills might get you a scholarship." Then he hastily added, "You can do this while receiving a very fine education."

That evening I shared the conversation with Judy. Her reaction was a predictable signal of support for whatever decision made me comfortable. She also trusted that my choice considered the welfare of the soon-to-be family of three. Playing football in a civilian setting with white players in 1955 was not in my thoughts, nor did I know how football scholarships worked. Furthermore, I didn't know any colored airmen who could tell me, and I never thought of asking one of the white former college players, including Coach Holmes.

Still, my foremost concern was how I would provide for my family. I was not yet educated, but I was eligible to re-enlist and retain a secure job with medical benefits for my family and a chance to see more of the world.

On January 25, 1955, we greeted our healthy son, James Christopher Alexander. Among the first sounds he could distinguish was my voice and he seemed to time his nap and awake in time for me to come home so that he could hear me enter and call his name and watch him smile. He was a good baby, seeming to behave as though trying to help us establish comfortable patterns for his care. He knew he was special, and he acknowledged our love in his bright eyes.

One day as I sat with my son on the bank of the San Antonio River, I remembered how, during my childhood, I often sat and watched the large clock in our hallway at home. Daddy observed my interest in the movement of the second hand, and I admitted that I couldn't decide if the very audible tick-tock signaled the future or announced the past. He said the answer might depend on whether you're expecting something to happen, or whether time passed and you missed an opportunity. I was holding my son, whose clock of life had just started. His immediate requirements would figure prominently in my decision. Whatever his opportunities in life, he was counting on his parents to provide what he needed to get started. I had come to another fork in the road. As always, the road behind closed yesterday. The map which led to the reenlistment office appeared more legible than the others, and I took that road.

Judy & Dorothea
Dow AFB

Father & son
San Antonio - 1955

Julia Porter

With James & Joycelyn
at church in
Orono, Maine - 1962

James Christopher
6 Months

James & Joycelyn
riding bike
in London - 1960

Judy, James
& Joycelyn - 1958

North Squad

IF THE SOUTH All-Stars lose a game this year it could be to the improving North All-Stars when the two six-man teams meets tonight at 7:30 in an intergroup football game. The North team, pictured above, includes l to r): first row: Manager Bud Hickey, Charlie Howard, Bill Williams, Bob Cornelius, Clarence Brown, Al Rose, Joe Johanns, Tom Sylvester and James Alexander. Second row—Coach Bob Holmes, Burnell Wimberly, Andy Tucker, Norwood Perry, Steve Smith, Allen Taylor, Jim Dotson, Louie Mullins, Frank Gardner, Bill Hansen, Lou Collette and Assistant Coach George Reichel. Not pictured are Tom Breeding, Jim Thompson, Pete Glover, Billy Hogg and Olando Simpson.

Starting Lineups

EAST	Pos.	NORTH
D. Kaufman, 200	LE	Al Rose, 225
J. Englert, 215	C	L. Mullins, 210
M. McDonald, 180	RE	J. Dotson, 175
K. Scheu, 175	QB	J. Alexander, 170
B. Pooley, 170	LH	L. Collette, 170
T. Wilkerson, 155	RH	F. Gardner, 215

The Alexander Family
1958

Another Life – Another Beginning

During a day in September, 1955, as we played with 9-month-old James Christopher, Judy whispered to him that he would soon have a sister or brother. He was such a happy child that he seemed to sense the importance of the announcement, and he definitely felt our excitement as we romped about and giggled. On the next day we bought another tape to measure the expansion of Judy's waistline.

At approximately 4:45 a.m., on June 27, 1956, Judy grunted and suggested we rush to the hospital. When I reached the maternity ward the nurses confirmed her caution. Less than an hour later, at 5:35 a.m., Joycelyn Louise Alexander opened her eyes. As I held my daughter, a stream of words and emotions engulfed me. Later that morning I wrote a lot of words on my note pad. I had not yet learned how to arrange the words, but on that day, and in that setting, life had a new meaning and I scribbled these words:

LIFE

Life is a journey that begins at the umbilical cord and stretches until the heart says --- amen. We do not determine the timing of either end, but in the interval, we learn; we forget. We love, and then we leave to sit with God and watch from above the sun rise on those who will surely follow.

My military obligation extended to 1961. But with the births of James Christopher and Joycelyn Louise my obligations to my family were of longer duration. Whatever the challenges of tomorrow I knew a better education would be an effective arsenal. Furthermore, I was still at Lackland where, each day on my drive to work, I passed the parade field and the spot where I painfully vowed to prepare myself for a better life.

On the day I visited the education office the only academic prerequisite I had for attending college was a high school diploma from a "separate and unequal" school. I had never taken a college entrance examination, nor did I have a transcript to apply for college admission. What I did have was a burning desire to educate myself. And so, on a night in September 1956 I walked into the admissions office of St. Mary's University. It was located among the satellite classrooms at nearby Kelly Air Force Base. When the administrator asked for my credentials and admissions paperwork, I simply pointed to myself and declared: "This is all I have. I want to leave here with more." We stood for a while in silence, both of us unsure how to proceed. And then he approached me; shook my hand and said, "Well, Sergeant, you picked a pretty good place to start. Come, let me give you the green light" He could not have used a more appropriate metaphor.

Pleading My Own Case

By September 1957, I had worked as a corpsman on general surgery, urology, obstetrics-gynecology, orthopedics, and neurosurgery wards and clinics. When I was assigned to surgery, the surgeons, anesthesiologists, nurses and fellow technicians rigorously trained me to be a very competent surgical technician. After seven years of service I was still a staff sergeant, and my path upward seemed blocked. During some of those years promotions were frozen due to a surplus of persons at my next grade level. But, no matter how hard I worked, my prospects of getting promoted were negligible until I received training at the School of Aviation Medicine (SAM). The person to hear my complaint was the Air Inspector, to whom; supposedly, confidential information could be disclosed, as well as gripes. I requested an appointment.

Even as I entered the room, I felt disconnected to the inspector. He was a major, and his posture projected superiority and formality, rather than creating an atmosphere of concern. His greeting:

Major: "What's on your mind, Sergeant?" It was a cold inquiry.

Sgt. Alexander: "Sir, my numerous requests for advanced medical training at the SAM have been ignored or discounted."

His reply was stern.

Major: "Maybe the training slots are going to others who outrank you."

Sgt. Alexander: Maybe you're right, Major, and if you are, then I'm entitled to know that's the reason. But, frankly, sir, those of us at this, the largest Air Force hospital, know that a disproportionate number of slots are going to smaller medical units, and that doesn't make sense to me.

Major: Making sense to you is not the concern of the Air Force as it formulates policy or allocates slots for training.

Sgt. Alexander: I think you're wrong, Major. I am a non-commissioned officer, responsible for implementing Air Force policy. If those policies don't make some sense to me, then I can't perform or supervise people to do stupid things.

Then I stood and looked directly into his eyes and politely recognized his authority:

Sgt. Alexander: "Sir, it just seems to me that anyone who has the authority to investigate and correct a stupid policy should get busy."

Major: That will be all, Sergeant.

For the next few weeks I controlled my disappointment by suggesting that the major might have been overwhelmed with complaints. After all, if all he heard all day is complaints, maybe after a while they all seemed alike. It was an attitude of generosity to assuage my own turmoil. It might have been more appropriate to suggest that he change his attitude, or change his job. But staff sergeants don't write performance reports for majors, so I went back to work and set a timetable for submitting another request.

At approximately 3 p.m., on December 24, 1957, I received an urgent phone call which summoned me to the Orderly Room. The clerk gave me orders to report to the SAM, located at Gunter AFB, Montgomery, Alabama, on January 2, 1958. Such assignments are generally known more than one hour before quitting time, one day before Christmas, and just nine days before the beginning of class. Ninety percent of the late notice wreaked the smell of revenge for my complaint to the Air Inspector. I was 95 percent certain that someone wanted me to request deferment to a later class -- which they would defer indefinitely. I was 100 percent determined to make the deadline, and to be an honor graduate after the 18 weeks of advanced training.

On Christmas day there was no mention to little James Christopher and Joycelyn Louise that they would play with their toys at another home in Alabama for five months. When they went to bed, Judy and I began dismantling our home, and before sundown the next day we were packing our belongings in a large U-Haul trailer. With our family relocated with Judy's loving and generous parents in Abbeville, Alabama, close enough for bi-weekly visits, I reported for class on New Year's Day, 1958.

Before the age of satellites, America maintained radar sites and other defense listening posts atop remote mountains and ice caps throughout the world. The School of Aviation Medicine trained good medical technicians to become super paramedics, who often became the only immediate medical person at those isolated stations. At the outset the doctors and administrators announced the strict requirements for graduation. Although my performance as a medic on a variety of wards, clinics and surgery was laudable, restructuring and expanding medical knowledge in an academic setting required different skills.

For the first two weeks of the four month course I struggled academically, until a friend offered a study regimen that she used as a college student. I also remembered the note taking and organization techniques the night nurse taught me a couple of years earlier. Both mentors demanded as repayment that I do my best.

I thought of both of them on May 16, 1958, the day I graduated – with honors.

The Ride Home

Those of us assigned to bases in Texas decided to convoy our private vehicles back home. There were six cars of uniformed colored, white and Hispanic personnel and dependents, some riding in vehicles other than their own. About an hour out of Montgomery we were stopped by the Alabama Highway Patrol, who disliked our integrated arrangement. They re-segregated our private vehicles and told us to get the hell out of Alabama. Within the next few miles our exodus was monitored at least twice as other patrols pulled alongside our caravan to ensure compliance. Shortly after we entered Mississippi, we stopped for refreshments at a gas station. Ironically, as we again selected our choices of integrated vehicles, we also chatted with two units of the Mississippi Highway Patrol, who wished us well and waved goodbye.

AIR UNIVERSITY
United States Air Force

SCHOOL OF AVIATION MEDICINE

BE IT KNOWN ___Staff Sergeant James E. Alexander, AF 14 447 661___ IS A GRADUATE OF

MEDICAL SERVICE TECHNICIAN COURSE

IN TESTIMONY WHEREOF, AND BY AUTHORITY VESTED IN US, WE DO CONFER
UPON HIM THIS DIPLOMA. GIVEN AT GUNTER AIR FORCE BASE, ALABAMA,
THIS ___16th___ DAY OF ___May___ 19 _51_ .

Walter L. Duff
COMMANDANT

Frank D. Hutchins
AIR UNIVERSITY LIBRARY

J. C. Strother
MAJOR GENERAL, USAF, COMMANDING

W. _____
MAJOR, USAF, SECRETARY AND REGISTRAR

Pledge

During part of my eight-year assignment at the Lackland Air Force Base hospital, I was Ward Master of the urology and a general surgical ward.

One day a patient asked me for additional help beyond the scope of my official duties. He was a master sergeant whose home station was Randolph Air Force Base, then the headquarters for world-wide personnel assignments and other major administrative affairs. I share our story here as I refer to him as Nick.

Nick anticipated a lengthy hospitalization, so when his wife arrived for her daily visit he asked me to join them for a special conference. He asked if I would be the primary respondent if his family needed anything during his absence from home. Even though Randolph was approximately 50 miles away along two lane highways in those days, I gave my assurances and informed my wife to expect a call from his wife and be ready to assist me if necessary. There never was a crisis that required my intervention, but my pledge gave him peace of mind.

Approximately three years after his discharge from the hospital, and after I had graduated from the SAM, the nurse summoned me for an urgent telephone call. The caller's memory was vivid. "Hey, Sergeant Alexander, this is Nick." We exchanged updates about our families and careers, and then he gave me bad news and good news. "Your name just came up for an assignment in Turkey, where you can't take your family. That's the bad news. The good news is that I'm in charge of world-wide medical technician assignments, so you and your family pack your bags for assignment at South Ruislip, England." For a moment I stood frozen. I also could not speak, because I heard another voice and felt another presence. Sergeant Robinson came briefly to smile and to remind me how those in charge can exercise their authority.

Finally, I asked, "Where is South England?"

He said, "You will love South Ruislip. It's located within 40 minutes to the center of London." Then he added, "Alex, I remember, when I needed you, you didn't hesitate. Thanks again."

End of conversation. We never spoke again.

Chapter Five: THE OLD WORLD AND A NEW DIRECTION

Rebirth

In November 1958 I preceded my family to England. Two months later, in January 1959, they were ready to join me, so I rented a house in North Harrow, Middlesex, a few blocks from Harrow; the internationally famous prep school. Before my departure to a base in Northern England to greet my family, I informed my new neighbors that I expected to return in two days with a wife and two children, ages 3 and 2. On the date of my scheduled return my new neighbors made frequent unsolicited entries into my home to light heaters and replenish the fuel and to place heated bricks in the beds to warm two small American children on their first night in an English winter. We settled into a community among neighbors unlike any we had known. How could we not feel welcome?

Within another month my life changed beyond my imagination. Nothing I had done prepared me for what would be, at age 24, not just another fork in the road, or even another highway, but a rebirth.

When I arrived at South Ruislip as a senior surgical technician, I was greeted by an outstanding medical team, so many who seemed upwardly mobile in their career. One physician was at the peak of his second career. He was such a quiet pleasant man, whose mere presence added a   special dignity to an assembly.

He also had the facility to remember, not only the names of his associates, but the names of their mates and children. He was a Southerner, so he appreciated my roots and often addressed me by my preference: Sergeant James Edward Alexander. He was Lieutenant Colonel James Van Pelt, M.D., Chief of Obstetrics & Gynecology. His other career ended 13 years earlier, on August 9, 1945, when he performed a different operation. Then, he was Captain James Van Pelt, navigator of the B-29 to Nagasaki.

One day, as I entered the surgical workroom, two other technicians read the Daily Bulletin. They laughed and joked about an announcement which invited interested persons to apply for duty with a special team called *On Target* (*OT*), which traveled to other bases throughout England, France, Germany, Scotland, and Norway. Both sergeants playfully emoted and expressed interest in applying. Because their qualifications equaled mine, I surmised that *On Target* must be a medical inspection team which visited other medical facilities. The Bulletin directed applicants to contact Mr. John Briley, a civilian employee, at Headquarters, Third Air Force, the building directly behind the hospital. I paid him a visit.

John Briley cordially greeted me and promptly asked, "Tell me about your acting experience."

I thought the question an unusual way to begin an interview about my medical training and experience, so I casually answered that my last performance was in the first grade. Furthermore, I proudly announced that I still remembered part of the song I sang as I wore a costume of a bear.

His eyes registered mild perplexity. Then he asked, "What do you think of *On Target*?"

I answered, "If it's on target it must be OK, since off-target signifies a miss." Though not amused, his eyes did acknowledge my witty response. Now we were both confused, so I openly declared, "I have no idea what you're talking about."

His gaze now signaled befuddlement and annoyance. He expressed both. "Sergeant Alexander your record shows that you have been here for three months. By your own admission you are unfamiliar with *On Target*, which means you have failed to attend three mandatory monthly sessions of Commanders Call."

My prompt reply was, "And I might miss the next one, unless you tell me what you're talking about, since it seems something was not covered in my incoming orientation."

As he fidgeted for an approach to preserve both of our dignities, we looked at each other and broke into such loud laughter that Joan, his secretary, entered and asked, in a most penetrating English accent, "Are you two daft?" – (a polite British way of asking, have you two lost your minds?)

My host then did something else unusual. He rose from his desk, walked over to me, extended his hand and said, "Let's start over. My name is Jack Briley. Can I call you Jim, or Alex?" I again gave permission to a temporary substitute for James Edward

Alexander. He then gave me a document of approximately 30 pages, which he said was a script. Only three months earlier the word script had entered my vocabulary as the money we Americans used to transact business on base. What he gave me was not money. Then he instructed me to read the lines after the bold name **STATZA,** and that he would read those after the bold name **DAVE**. Suddenly, the telephone rang. The call was for Jack, but the call might well have been the most important telephone call of my military career; possibly for the re-direction of my life, and the caller didn't even know my name.

After no more than three minutes, Jack finished his conversation and redirected his attention to me. He began reading Dave's lines. I responded as Statza. We finished the first page. Before he turned to page 2, he paused and gave me a strange look. In the middle of page 2 he stopped and gave me a longer stare, but he remained silent. In the middle of page 3 he paused again, then asked, "How long have you been doing that?"

Equally puzzled, I asked, "Doing what? And why am I reading this?"

He explained his surprise. "You are not reading. You are delivering those lines from memory. Within the time span of my telephone conversation you apparently memorized three pages of dialogue. Now tell me, how long have you been able to do that?"

I faced him directly and declared, "I have absolutely no idea what happened, how it happened, or your purpose." He gave me some answers.

In 1953 John Briley was studying in England for a Ph.D. in Elizabethan drama. When he reported for reserve duty at Headquarters Third Air Force, his writing and communications skills landed him in the Office of the Directorate of Information. He and another talented officer, Lieutenant Wilson Brydon, convinced their superiors that some of the information commanders wanted disseminated to the troops could be efficiently delivered in a novel "theatrical" fashion by regular GIs portraying characters within the tragedy-comedy spectrum. Briley further suggested that following his two-week tour of duty as a reserve officer, he should continue in a newly created position as civilian employee to write the scripts, direct the "actors" and administer the innovative program. It was a case of the employee creating his job.

With cautious approval from his superiors, Jack Briley searched the records for military personnel, regardless of rank, who had some acting experience. Among the GIs who answered the call were Airman Larry Hagman, and Army Private Frank Gorshin.

Larry Hagman was in England as a member of the cast of *South Pacific*, which starred his mother, Mary Martin. When he entered the Air Force, he was assigned to a "Special Services" unit and continued to produce and direct entertainment for the troops. Frank Gorshin was a 19-year-old soldier in 1953 who also was a Special Services entertainer serving in England. Both young GIs were part of the original *On Target* team, long before Larry recited lines as JR Ewing on the television show *Dallas*, or before Frank's role as The Riddler in *Batman*. They also had finished their military service before I knew their names. Other GIs had replaced them, and now Briley was auditioning approximately 75 persons to fill a new vacancy on the team. Our interview was not going well. We cordially said goodbye and I returned to my duties in surgery.

Another announcement on the bulletin board listed a two week management course, scheduled to begin the following Monday. Three days later I went to class.

After the last day of the course, I wondered who had been selected to fill the actor vacancy. My curiosity guided me to Jack's office. And, almost as if scripted, as I approached his door, Joan exited and said, "Sergeant Alexander, you should go straight away to your mail box." There, attached to a large package was a document which boldly stated MILITARY ORDER, followed by language which directed that Staff Sergeant Alexander, James E., be immediately assigned to The Directorate of Information, Headquarters, Third Air Force.

Before opening the envelope I stood for a long time motionless and silent, so long that another surgical technician touched me and asked, "Where are you?"

My truthful reply was, "I don't know. I have just been selected for the *On Target* team.

In typical GI fashion he said, "No s---! Congratulations."

Then I opened the envelope and was notified that the team was on two week "down time", and that my immediate reassignment also excused me from duty for that period. However, Briley ordered that I take the time to become familiar with the enclosed three scripts and be ready for the first reading upon return to duty. Next, I went straight away home and tried to explain to Judy what *On Target* was, which I had never seen, and what my new job would be, which was not what I was trained to do.

When we assembled for rehearsals, the first order of business was for Jack to introduce me as the newest member. Two names were already familiar from the audition script. The stocky civilian said in a very deep voice, "I be Dave. Welcome to *On Target.*" He was David Healy, a professional actor trained by B. Iden Payne at the University of Texas. Dave hated to memorize lines, and detested rehearsals more. Yet he was a master at knowing the true meaning of a script and would extemporize through most performances with appropriate remarks. Another hand was extended with the announcement, "I'm Airman Second Class James Statza. I like girls. Do you have a sister?" Even if he had been wearing civilian clothes, Statza's natural manner was a neon sign which read GI. He was frequently mistaken for the real actor Peter Sellers, because they shared a striking physical resemblance. Waiting quietly and patiently was Airman First Class Ellis Fortune, another Texan. At the end of the day my management and supervisory skills detected that Ellis was a good actor, and that he was the one member who kept track of all costumes and equipment.

Within the next few weeks I was introduced to a world beyond the scope of ordinary military exposure. Jack defined my new duties: In addition to learning and performing my roles on stage, I was required to read the daily edition of *The Manchester Guardian* and *The London Times* newspapers, both of which were new to me. As we travelled in chauffeured staff cars to bases throughout England and flew on specially assigned planes throughout Europe and Scandinavia, we played games that tested our knowledge and memory. There was so much that I didn't know. So, again, I carried a pad to note what needed to be learned, and when the others were asleep I studied my notes; preparing to keep the promise I made to myself a decade ago on the parade field.

To help me learn the craft of acting, I was given tickets and assigned the "duty" of attending various shows in London's West End theatre district to observe professionals at work. Briley told me to learn the directions to The Old Vic, The Royal Haymarket Theatre, Drury Lane, Covent Garden Opera House, and The Royal Albert Hall. Furthermore, since our monthly travels took us near The Royal Shakespeare Theatre at Stratford-upon-Avon, Briley also ordered tickets for me to attend and learn from performances of *King Lear, Coriolanus, The Merchant of Venice, Richard III,* and *Troilus and Cressida.* I also attended a most memorable performance of *Othello,* starring Paul Robeson, as the Moor, Mary Ure, as Desdemona, and Sam Wanamaker, as Iago. In addition, to improve my speech delivery, Jack arranged for me to have private speech lessons from a teacher who also was assisting William Holden and Nancy Kwan. They were in London filming *The World of Suzie Wong.*

We also scheduled breaks so that we could spend time in the real world. During one such period I accepted another challenge. Cambridge University invited all American forces located throughout Europe to select 25 persons to attend a special two-week course in international relations. I applied and was accepted. The road to *On Target* intersected with the road to Cambridge, and I took that fork to a most exhilarating academic experience.

I was the only married member of *On Target,* spending Monday to Friday away from home. To reconnect with my family I periodically took breaks from the team and returned to the surgical suite. Another reason for the interruption was to stay current in my specialty, which determined my eligibility for promotions. I was still a staff sergeant approaching my tenth year of service. A new urgency boosted my need for advancement.

In September 1960, Judy fixed June 1961 for the arrival of our third child. Kenneth Anthony didn't disappoint his mother's schedule; he arrived on June 30. At birth he opened his eyes, seemingly just to announce his presence, and he took a very long nap for a few days, as if taking an extended vacation at birth.

Four days later, July 4th, just before joining the American Independence Day celebrations on the base, I visited my son in the nursery. When I held him he opened his eyes, and it seemed he asked me a question: 'Dad, how and where will you take care of me?'

And now we were a family of five. Eight days before Kenneth's birth I had prepared for his question and followed a familiar sign to the reenlistment office. We extended our tour of active duty another six years. At the end of this enlistment I will have served for 16 years. We all knew I would stay and retire after 20 years, at age 37. Now, I had to project beyond my days in uniform.

On Target had guided me into an adventurous world where almost everything I did was outside the channels of the entire armed forces. Within the scope of so many new and varied roles and assignments, I was trained to think and speak differently. I paid careful attention to John Briley, the most organized and articulate person I had ever met. One month as he prepared to vacation with his family, he wrote four scripts for *On Target*, added significantly to his thesis for a PhD, and performed his regular duties as the Director of Orientation Activities at Third Air Force Headquarters. It was a performance worth emulating.

And then, it was time to return to the United States.

(John Briley continued to write scripts. In 1982 he won the Academy Award for writing the Best Original Screenplay for the movie Gandhi.)

You Need a Passport to Take the Off Ramp

In one *On Target* skit we urged servicemen with families to insure that their dependent's passports were updated at least 6 months before returning to the United States. Parents of children born outside the continental United States were urged to obtain a Certificate of Birth Abroad, which is essential to verify the newborn's citizenship upon return to the U.S. Shortly after our son Kenneth was born in June 1961, I followed the procedures and secured all necessary documents for our return.

Seven months later, January 1962, movers came and packed our household goods for prompt shipment to our next assignment at Dow AFB, Maine. We packed the essentials for a family of five to travel and moved to a hotel to await ground transportation to another base for our flight home. At approximately 10:00 a.m., on the morning before our scheduled departure from the London area, Judy and I decided to make one last run through our travel checklist. As each item was mentioned, either she or I would say "check" to confirm completion or possession.

We started: all pound sterling changed to U.S. dollars, check; military orders and travel vouchers, check; sufficient baby bottles with formula, check; passports, silence; passports, silence. Within the next three minutes we searched everywhere and each other, and rightfully concluded they were indeed in a safe place ---

in our household goods. To avoid the appearance of panic in the presence of our children, now ages 6, 5, and seven months, I very calmly asked Judy to prepare the family for a ride downtown to the American Embassy. That was a strange request, since our car was also among the goods already shipped. I closed the door and had a very serious talk with God, and then I made two urgent telephone calls; first, to the passport clerk at the base to request copies of my entire passport file, and a second call to borrow a car.

Shortly after noon we entered the American Embassy. Without fanfare or stutter, I announced to the receptionist, "My name is Sergeant James Edward Alexander. This is my family. We are due to fly home day after tomorrow. Our passports are in our household goods, and they are aboard a cargo ship in the middle of the Atlantic. Now, please let me speak with someone who can help me, even if you have to call Ambassador David Bruce."

Just then a man, who overheard my plea, calmly walked over to us and said to me, "Do you actually think we can issue you a new passport in one day?"

I calmly answered, "I do believe it can be done, and this is where I should begin."

Another ten seconds passed with our eyes locked, but neither of us speaking. Then, as though struck by a thunderbolt from Zeus, he became very excited and issued some orders: Give me your paper work. Go directly to a passport photographer (he provided the directions), bring the picture back to me, then take your family to a movie, and return here at 2:30 P.M." Then he smiled and said, "You are one lucky fellow. My job is taking care of such emergencies."

Thirty minutes later I put the pictures in the official's hand. We decided to forego the movies, and chose to walk around London for a final tourist visit.

At 2:25 we returned to Grosvenor Square, and climbed the steps under the giant eagle resting atop the front of the Embassy. As we opened the door, the official handed me an envelope and told me to examine the contents. After my inspection, we just looked at each other and nodded our heads. As we turned to go, I searched for words to express our appreciation. Three words were sufficient. I simply said, "God bless America."

Dave explaining his dream

Statza and Lamb pleading innocence

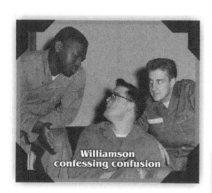

Williamson confessing confusion

Leaving for Norway

Relaxing in Oslo

SSgt. 1958

CITATION TO ACCOMPANY THE AWARD OF
THE AIR FORCE COMMENDATION MEDAL

TO
JAMES E. ALEXANDER

Staff Sergeant James E. Alexander distinguished himself as Noncommissioned Officer In Charge of the "On Target" Information and Ground Training Program of Headquarters Third Air Force, South Ruislip, England, from 11 May 1959 to 10 October 1960. During his service as Noncommissioned Officer In Charge of the team, and as an actor thereon, he mastered all duties outstandingly, and his great personal integrity, his amiability and his qualities of leadership were instrumental in welding together a team of unusual merit. As an actor he put relentless effort into perfecting his diction, his characterizations, and his method of presentation, acquiring and outstanding capacity to communicate mood and message to large audiences under very difficult conditions. As leader of a team that traveled many hundreds of miles each month performing under a grueling schedule, he was a dynamic source of strength on stage and off. During his tenure as NCOIC, the "On Target" team was invited to perform in Germany, France, and Norway and had a string of unusually successful programs. The outstanding example Sergeant Alexander set, the exceptional quality of his leadership, and the contribution as a performer figured prominently in the attainment of this record. Through his meritorious service, Sergeant Alexander has reflected the highest credit upon himself and the United States Air Force.

Chapter Six: ROLL THE DICE; SOMETIMES YOU WIN

Lows and Highs

Within a month after arriving at Dow AFB, Bangor, Maine, I became disenchanted for the first time in my military career. My interest in the medics had waned since *On Target* ignited a broader range of interests and skills. Even though I outranked the sergeant who supervised the operating room, his enthusiasm for the job was greater than mine, so I asked the nurse supervisor to retain him in that job. She offered me the job of supervising Central Supply, the section which prepared and dispensed sterile supplies for the entire hospital. Although it was an important job in the hospital chain, going to work was difficult.

Two months later, as I pondered how my lack of interest would eventually impact my performance, I answered the telephone with little enthusiasm: "Central supply; Sergeant Alexander."

The caller responded: "Well I'll be damn. Are you Jim Alexander who was with *On Target* in England?" Just the mention of *OT* filled me with momentary delight, thinking how, unlike now, I once loved my job. Even before I could disengage from my instant reverie, the caller identified himself.

"Jim, I'm Wil Brydon; you must have heard Jack Briley mention my name." He was   now Captain Brydon, assigned to the Directorate of Information, Headquarters Eighth Air Force, located at Westover AFB, Springfield, Massachusetts.

My response was to cite his history, as I remembered it. "Jack told me you helped organize the original *OT* team. He also said you're a very bright man, but occasionally lazy as shit about details that must be attended for an operation such as *OT*."

He laughed and actually confirmed: "Well, that's part of why I called you. How would you like to come to Westover and help me organize another *OT*?" Jack Briley knew that performing in and supervising a road show required a certain temperament and special supervisory skills. Wil Brydon admitted that Jack withheld permission to use the original *OT* scripts until he could locate and persuade me to assist his efforts. Wil offered to drive from Springfield to Bangor, Maine, the following Sunday to personally meet me.

Three weeks later Captain Brydon and I finished auditions and began rehearsals at Westover, a base of the Strategic Air Command (SAC). Suddenly, in the middle of rehearsals, there was a world-wide readiness exercise at all SAC bases. The base theater where we rehearsed was needed for briefings. Before the sun set, Wil Brydon had worked his magic and obtained permission for us to use the theaters at two of the nearby "Seven Sisters" colleges -- Smith College at Northampton, and Mount Holyoke College at South Hadley.

We performed at all Eighth Air Force bases, and at Headquarters Second Air Force, before taking the stage at Offutt AFB, SAC Headquarters at Omaha, Nebraska. Our last performance was in September 1962, and we awaited approval to form a new *OT* team.

Before departing Westover, I told Captain Brydon that I really didn't want to return to my job as a medic. He thought of a plan, which if successful, would instantly channel me into a new career. Anything with that much potential requires careful thought, precise planning and flawless execution --- a situation fit for Wilson Brydon, the master planner. We rehearsed our "script" and I returned to Dow.

At approximately 0845 the next day, I casually walked into the medical squadron Orderly Room to report my return from temporary duty at Eighth Air Force Headquarters -- where the generals work. As I stood chatting with the executive officer, a lieutenant colonel, and the sergeant major, a senior master sergeant, the telephone rang. A clerk informed the officer: "The line has a lot of static, but it sounds like a general from Eighth Air Force Headquarters." All I heard after that was the colonel's voice: "Good morning sir. Yes sir, he's here in the Orderly Room right now, sir. Yes sir. Yes sir. We'll take care of it sir."

On a telephone line, temporarily impaired by static or something else that I really didn't want to know, Captain Wilson Brydon must have sounded like a general who requested that I be transferred forthwith to the Directorate of Information at Dow. My new director at the higher command would be, of course, Captain Brydon. Orders for my transfer were dictated by the colonel and prepared by the sergeant major.

Before departing the hospital I went to every ward, clinic, service and department, to say goodbye to some of the finest colleagues one could expect in a lifetime.

After 11 years I was changing course again; detouring into a world more suited for me to develop new talents for better service today, and for more marketable employment tomorrow. I had worked hard to achieve senior status in two medical specialties. Now, I would have to start at the bottom of a new career, learning the fundamentals of journalism, broadcasting, and public affairs. But I also inventoried my assets: My family, an eagerness to learn, and the rank of NCO with knowledge of the "system."

It was a busy day. When I arrived at home and told Judy how it happened, her only question was: "When they shoot Captain Brydon, will they also shoot you?"

One month later, in October 1962, the world's attention shifted to the performance of two super powers flexing their nuclear armed military muscles and making speeches in what history records as the Cuban Missile Crisis. That debacle dashed our hopes and dreams of ever organizing another *O T* team. It also threatened to dash the hopes of humanity.

Higher Profiles and Tensions

When I transferred to the Directorate of Information, Master Sergeant John Marra was in charge. According to some reports, he was the only enlisted Director of Information in the Strategic Air Command, and according to all reports he was the best historian in the Air Force. Shortly after my arrival, he was reassigned to another base to document Air Force participation in the Cuban Missile Crisis.

Three days before his departure he drove me to the office of the Wing Commander and requested that I be designated his replacement, even though I had no formal training as an information specialist. When the commander reminded him that there were two NCOs who outranked me, with experience, Sergeant Marra cited my writing and communications proficiency and assured the commander that I was also a better supervisor than the others. Furthermore, the other sergeants also endorsed my appointment.

The commander walked over to me and stood almost eyeball-to-eyeball, and said, "Sergeant Alexander, Sergeant Marra just paid you one of the highest compliments you're likely to get in the Air Force. I trust his judgment. Now, go do it." Upon our return to the office the two other NCOs greeted me and promised their full support, even though their refusals to take charge dimmed their prospects for promotion.

One officer openly expressed his disappointment that he was not selected for the high profile position as the commander's spokesman to the public, especially the media. He was especially incensed that an enlisted man held the position. The commander calmly reminded the officer that not all intelligent airmen wear bars. Furthermore, he observed that there were more college educated enlisted airmen in the Directorate of Information than in any office on base, and that two of them had earned degrees that exceeded those of the frustrated officer. The Directorate was responsible for conducting the public affairs program within the Bangor community, producing the weekly base newspaper, gathering information classified as SECRET and TOP SECRET to write the official history of the organizations, which included B-52 bombers and aerial tankers on full military alert. It was where the commander stood with us on several occasions to greet frequent visitors, U.S. Senators Margaret Chase Smith, and Edward S. Muskie.

Does a B-52 Bomber Fly Low?

Less than three months after I assumed duties at the information office, a B-52 bomber crashed in the heavily wooded area of Maine. All ears tuned to the Dow for information. It was where reporters came for briefings and updates.

Westover Air Force Base was home to the crew of the downed plane, so there was special interest in the Springfield, Massachusetts, community to identify the crew and their status. Since B-52 bombers carry nuclear weapons, national and international audiences also wanted to know if such weapons were aboard. Incidents of this magnitude are generally handled by experienced, senior trained spokespersons, so, Colonel Bill Fendall, Deputy Chief of Information for Eighth Air Force came to take charge. When a reporter from United Press International (UPI) directed his question to the senior officer, the colonel politely referred him to me for his answers. Throughout the next three days the officer monitored and applauded my management of this incident, as he sent constant updates back to headquarters.

Then, we got a telephone call from a radio station that served the Westover audience. Although both the colonel and I listened on separate phones, he motioned me to answer the questions. One sensitive question concerned the altitude of the plane just before the crash, since training flights were conducted at various altitudes.

To capture the flavor of "Action News," the radio announcer informed his audience: "I'm talking live with the information office at Dow Air Force Base in Maine."

After answering all the questions I could, the announcer asked what altitude the plane was flying before the crash. I promised the announcer that a board of inquiry would convene to determine the cause of the accident, and their findings would be shared with the public, to the extent that national security concerns permit.

Colonel Fendall smiled his approval. Just as I expected the conversation to end, the announcer reopened the sensitive altitude issue. He asked, "Does a B 52 ever fly low?"

My answer exposed both impatience and fatigue: I blurted: "Shit, all planes fly low; immediately after they take off, and immediately before they land. Now shut up."

The officer's roar of laughter shook the walls. There were no more inquiries that day.

When the crash crisis was over and before Colonel Fendall returned to Westover, he admitted that he searched my files and learned that I was rated as both a Senior Medical Technician and a Senior Surgical (Operating Room) Technician. He said, "You are one hot property. Some medical group would just love to get a dual qualified senior technician, but I've got you now, and I'm not letting you go."

And then he asked: "Sergeant Alexander, I want you to do me a favor." He explained that the Department of Defense was considering creating the Defense Information School to consolidate all journalism, broadcasting, and public affairs training. His office was asked to explore the efficacy of such a consolidation. He then asked me to attend the present Army Information School, located at Ft. Slocum, NY, and to give him a critique and my recommendation.

A few days before I left for school, I answered a telephone call from Colonel Fendall: "Sergeant Alexander, I expect that you will perform as well in journalism at Ft. Slocum, as you did in the Medical Service Technician Course at the Air University School of Aviation Medicine in 1958, and at the special course in International Relations at Cambridge."

That is how colonels get what they want: They let you *know* how much they *know*, so that you don't say *no*.

Prayer Changes Things

I enjoyed my new job, but Maine was just too cold and had too much snow. But if that's what you've got; that's what you use. One day I looked for a hill where James Christopher and Joycelyn could use their newly purchased sled. We found the perfect spot --- a Bangor city street. I was not the only one who thought the site was too good to abandon, so a policeman simply blocked off the street so that they could romp for a while. Joycelyn still cites that day as one of her best childhood memories.

Then, on September 16, 1962, Dorothea Marie joined the family. Her coming also spurred us to review the new numbers. She made us a family of 6; 15 months after the birth of Kenneth; and as I began my 11th year of service --- less than 10 years from retirement. I was still a staff sergeant (E-5). But Dorothea also brought some specials. Even as she lay in her basinet, she seemed to have entered the world under a canopy of calmness. She and her serenity were my new gifts. My spirits were raised, and I reassessed the positives. Military life provided some pleasant constants. We had a job, a decent and safe home environment, and our children attended good, safe schools. As for promotions, I would continue to perform at the highest level – and pray. I remembered my grandmother's often repeated declaration of surety. "Prayer changes things."

Within a month the Wing Commander, Colonel James Flanagan, entered the information office with a look on his face that signaled a problem. He stated his concerns: "Gentlemen, because of slow promotions, I sense a possible morale problem among our NCOs, and I need your help." He was almost preaching to the choir. Dow AFB was a front-line base of the Strategic Air Command, where high morale and high performance were essential. Colonel Flanagan's plea: "You men know that this shortage of promotions won't last forever, and when it's over, those persons who maintained high performance through this drought will obviously be promoted first. So, since you fellows comprise the largest pool of creative thinkers in a single office, I need you to put your heads together and give me some creative ideas to raise morale." Then, looking at me, as the supervisor, he walked over to our chalkboard and wrote the word <u>MORALE</u>, then smiled and said: "Is that OK with you, Sergeant Alexander?"

In GI jargon, whenever someone reveals to you what you thought was your secret, they are said to have "peeped your hole card." We had a secret that we thought was confined to our office. Each day, one of us would write at least five words on the chalk board. Throughout the day this pool of creative talent would write newspaper articles and top secret histories of operational activities. But before we departed for the day, there also was a special basket in which to drop at least half a dozen dirty jokes using the five words on the board in the punch line. Through some grapevine,

Colonel Flanagan had "peeped our dirty joke hole card." Our commander was asking us to divert some intellectual energy into something worthwhile. He heard our very loud applause, and he joined our roar of laughter.

Two days later I asked the commander to revisit our office. We presented him a sample pamphlet cover, adorned with chevrons and the words: HOW TO GET PROMOTED. Everyone knew that top rated performance reports, medals and decorations, longevity, etc., influenced one's chances for advancement, so we asked Colonel Flanagan what additional qualities would be considered.

His answer was quick and forthright: "As commander, I will promote to the next higher grade, the noncommissioned officer who is designated the Outstanding NCO of the Half Year."

We stood, saluted, and I said, "Thank you sir. We'll take it from here."

Three days later we delivered to the commander 10,000 pamphlets which outlined tips for improving one's chances for promotion. In a separate section we detailed the incentive and the process for being selected Noncommissioned Officer of the Half Year. When I arrived home that day, I also presented a pamphlet to Judy and then stroked my staff sergeant chevrons and declared, "This June, I plan to give myself a special birthday present of technical sergeant stripes, by becoming the Outstanding Noncommissioned Officer of the Half Year of 1963."

Approximately 3,000 sergeants knew the competition for outstanding NCO also required the candidate to appear before at least three boards of senior officers to be quizzed about military customs and courtesies and explain how to supervise complex hypothetical management scenarios.

Three months after we published the pamphlet and the competition ended, Colonel Flanagan came to our office with a special message: "I want to express my appreciation for the fine job you guys did on the brochure. Thank you." Then he turned to me and asked a very personal question: "Sergeant Alexander is there something Mrs. Alexander asked you to bring home from the commissary?" My non-verbal expression clearly signaled 'why are you asking that question?' Sensing that, he offered: "Well, when you do go near the commissary, walk across the street to the clothing sales store and pick up a set of technical sergeant stripes. Congratulations, Sergeant Alexander, you are the Outstanding Noncommissioned Officer of the Half Year for the 397th Bombardment Wing. Every officer of the boards sends congratulations and expressions of respect." Amid the very loud applause from all hands, the colonel turned to me, smiled and added: "Alex, you're something special. I'm proud to have you in my command. By the way, you don't have to deliver to me the dirty jokes you guys wrote using the word morale." I escorted him to his car. Before I re-entered the building I took a short stroll and wiped my eyes.

That evening when the family sat for dinner, I casually sauntered around the table, and in a casual gesture I tossed a set of new technical sergeant chevrons on the table and acknowledged the contribution of the entire family: "See what we did. Thanks." When the clapping and immediate celebration subsided I recounted for my children the power of having a goal, self discipline, hard work, and my grandfather's reminder: "Success or failure in life is more often determined by what you do for yourself than what others do to you or for you."

Another award for being the NCO of the Half Year was to join selected outstanding air crews and persons from other Eighth Air Force bases for a trip to Cape Canaveral to watch the launch of a satellite. Our host was Brigadier General Harry James Sands, Jr. Weather conditions postponed the launch, but General Sands gave us a tour of the facilities.

At one stop near a large hanger he walked over to me, put his hand on my name tag and spoke: "Sergeant Alexander, so you're the Outstanding Non-commissioned Officer for your wing. Congratulations." Then he smiled and observed, "You must be pretty good. Just how good are you?"

Without hesitation I answered, "Sir, I am as good in my job as you are in yours." He flashed a big grin and said, "Damn, if that's the case, you're good." He then looked me squarely in the eyes and offered his salute.

Broadcast School

On my last day of journalism school at the Army Information School, the broadcast instructors said they expected to see me again. Eighteen months later, the Air Force allowed me to gain new talents by attending the Broadcast Specialist Course at the newly chartered Defense Information School, (DINFOS). Broadcasting had attracted me since the day, in 1953, when I joined a group of men at Lackland in the recitation of the rosary, live, on a San Antonio radio station. Sometimes the forks in the road converge.

It is a long drive from Bangor, Maine to New Rochelle, New York. As I took that journey in October 1964, I also pondered where my newly acquired skills would be used in the Armed Forces Radio & Television Service (AFRTS). Except for the largest military hospitals in this country, all broadcast operations by AFRTS are conducted outside the United States, to provide information, education, and entertainment to American armed forces. At some small bases and aboard ships, families are not allowed to accompany broadcasters to their assignments. My wish list was for a station in Japan, Germany, or the Philippines, where our family could experience another foreign tour together.

Throughout the eight weeks of training our class comprised a mixture of ranks and talents from all branches of the armed forces. Part of the final examination was a two-day exercise in which each student performed in a variety of positions in a radio and television station. Three days before the exercise the instructors selected two persons, regardless of rank, as "Station Managers," one for radio and one for television. It is a prestigious position which recognizes the student's academic and leadership skills. For Radio Station Manager, the instructors selected an airman second class (E-3). He organized his station, and we followed his directions. For Television Station Manager, they selected Technical Sergeant James Edward Alexander.

One of the most critically graded elements of the Broadcast Exercise was a segment of exactly four minutes and fifty nine seconds (04:59). All members of the crew contributed ideas for the subject by selecting and volunteering to write the feature and finding the right graphics.

Someone offered an idea for the subject: "What about the Commandant, Colonel John J. Christy. He is one of the most decorated veterans of World War II. I heard he went AWOL from his hospital bed to join his buddies in the Battle of the Bulge."

My immediate response was, "I want to know why anybody would do that. I'll go ask him."

When I announced myself and requested to see the Commandant, he heard my voice and immediately invited me into his office. His greeting was forthwith: "Come in, Station Manager. Congratulations." For a few seconds I just stood and looked at him, until he asked, "Is there something wrong, Sergeant?"

Then I answered, "Sir, the story is that you were already wounded but left your hospital bed to join your comrades in the Battle of the Bulge. It also is my understanding that you don't talk much about that experience. Sir, not too many persons are that … ah … are that …"

He interrupted: "Is *crazy* the word you're looking for?"

I nodded and answered: "Sir, that's a good start."

He remained silent for about 15 seconds, then turned sharply and gestured for me to load a tape on the recorder and take a seat. That session still ranks as the top interview of my broadcast career. Ordinary guys don't do what he did, but his explanation was plain and simple. "That's what warriors do for each other; otherwise, everybody perishes."

Now we needed graphics, so I asked the colonel if we could use some photos from his collection. This brave man, who had just described his brush with death, openly declared, "All of the pictures are kept by Mrs. Christy, and I'm not that brave to suggest she part with them." After much more pleading on my part, he finally offered to at least "raise the subject."

Later, in the early evening, a soldier came to my room and announced Mrs. Christy's invitation to join her for coffee. She was a slight lady with a gentle smile, but despite her warm greeting, some instinct told me to be careful. We started a dialogue:

Mrs. Christy: Congratulations on being selected as Station Manager for the Broadcast Exercise.

Alexander: Thank you ma'am, but you could make my job easier if you let me borrow your pictures.

In the distance I heard a door open, and I also heard Mrs. Christy say aloud, "John, come back here. I have a message for both of you." She continued:

Mrs. Christy: Sergeant Alexander, our exciting family history is pictured in these four albums. They have never been out of my possession. I repeat; they have never been out of my possession. Now, you want me to trust you with this valuable treasure. [Then she turned to put both the colonel and me in clear focus. He and I shifted and squirmed a little, and she continued:]

Mrs. Christy: There is something about you that I want to trust, and so I'm going to let you use these albums. I know the location of every picture in every album. If they are not returned to me in the same order and condition, you and John should make reservations for the ferry. [Ft. Slocum was located on an island off the coast near New Rochelle, accessed only by the ferry.]

That night I didn't sleep much. The albums rested near my pillow. When I saw the colonel the next day, I could not resist reminding him. "Sir, I was aware that my war hero was trying to sneak out the back door last evening, thus leaving me without a comrade."

He said, "The Battle of the Bulge was somewhat easier; this lady takes no prisoners." It was a good day. I had met a tough guy and a tougher lady.

Some graduates were immediately informed of their next assignment. As I prepared myself for graduation the next day, Sergeant Bill Harvey, an instructor, paid a visit to my room. Bill was another Southerner from Alabama, so we related to each other at a closer level.

He began the conversation with a grin and a chuckle and said, "You performed your ass off so well as station manager yesterday, that you also got yourself a special assignment." Bill then led me to the office of Lieutenant Colonel Shale "Bud" Tulin, the Air Force Liaison Officer.

Colonel Tulin got right to the point: "Sergeant Alexander, congratulations on your performance as station manager in the final exercise yesterday. Now, I need a big favor."

When a colonel asks a sergeant for a favor, most sensible sergeants simply ask, "What, sir?" or "When, sir?" I looked at him and asked, "In exchange for what?"

Three men stood dancing and laughing like schoolboys, until Tulin put his hand on my shoulder and said, "Alex, I'll make it up to you." He informed me that they urgently needed a replacement station manager at Sondrestrom, Greenland. There was something so sincere about his manner that I simply shook his hand and said, "It's a deal, Colonel."

Colonel Tulin then placed a telephone call to another sergeant in the personnel assignment section at Randolph AFB. His message was brief: "Sergeant Alexander will take the Greenland assignment. We will owe him a big one."

Graduate, Broadcast Specialist Course

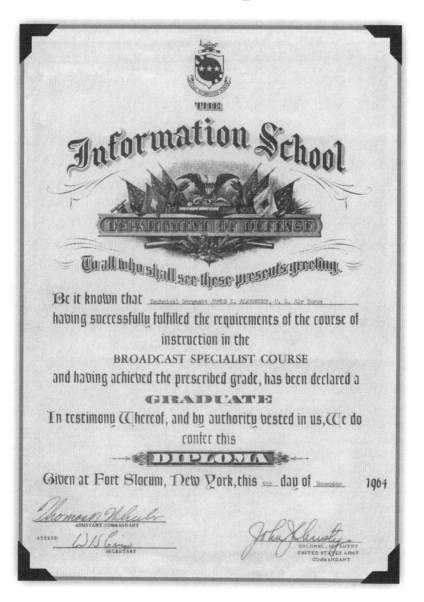

THE

Information School

DEPARTMENT OF DEFENSE

To all who shall see these presents greeting.

Be it known that ~~Technical Sergeant JAMES E. ALEXANDER, U. S. Air Force~~
having successfully fulfilled the requirements of the course of
instruction in the

BROADCAST SPECIALIST COURSE

and having achieved the prescribed grade, has been declared a

GRADUATE

In testimony Whereof, and by authority vested in us, We do
confer this

DIPLOMA

Given at Fort Slocum, New York, this 6th day of November 1964

_____
ASSISTANT COMMANDANT

ATTEST: _____
SECRETARY

_____
COLONEL, INFANTRY
UNITED STATES ARMY
COMMANDANT

Promises

A few weeks before I left for school, James Christopher asked for a ride to the Ford dealership in Bangor, where he entered the annual Ford Pass, Punt & Kick contest. He also asked me to help him prepare for competition, and he then invited other boys in the neighborhood to join our practice sessions. At the completion of the local contest, Maine officials said his scores were so high that they declared him the 9-Year-Old Maine State Champion, and asked him to represent the state for the New England title. We gave each other mutual promises: he promised to do his best. I promised to be there with him.

Coincidently, the date for competition at Fenway Park in Boston was the same date of my graduation from the Broadcast Specialist Course at Ft. Slocum, near New York City, a considerable distance apart. He was escorted to Boston by an official of the contest who lived in Bangor. Even though military brats are conditioned to schedule conflicts in which preference is given to military related functions, my son knew I would also do my best to keep my promise.

Red lights always get attention, especially when they're flashing atop the vehicle behind you. State highway patrolmen have a way of asking the right question to let drivers give the wrong answer. But, seeing my military uniform, the officer simply said: "You tell me why you're speeding."

155

After explaining how my military graduation ceremony created time conflicts with my promise to my nine-year-old son to get to Boston for his PP&K competition, the patrolman just stood in silence. Then he told me to listen very carefully, and he said, "I don't want you speeding on New York highways. But, it just happens that I'm heading to the state line, and I plan to travel pretty fast. If I look in the rear view mirror and see you behind me, you're not speeding." He then parted the traffic for a very fast and thoughtful escort. When we approached the Connecticut border he again flashed his lights and pulled over to allow me to proceed, and for us to exchange salutes.

My son did his best. I watched him perform. He slept for most of the drive from Boston to Bangor, --- holding my diploma from The Broadcast Specialist Course.

The Rock

After re-settling my family from base quarters to a civilian community in Bangor, my one year tour in Greenland began in January 1965. When I stepped from the plane at approximately 9:15 P.M., an airman quickly approached and draped a parka over my shoulder and offered, "Welcome to 'The Rock.' It's approximately 44 degrees below zero." He then pointed to his name tag which read CURTIS, and he added, "I'm Chris, Mrs. Curtis' boy." Chris Curtis had a car waiting to rush me to the station, a building sitting atop the highest hill on the base, and dubbed "The Castle."

Within 15 minutes of landing I greeted my crew. Even though this was my first assignment as a Broadcast Specialist, the team offered me the courtesy of directing the live newscast, scheduled to begin in less than 30 minutes. It did not matter that I had just endured a long propeller-driven plane ride from New Jersey, in turbulence most of the way, and with stops in Newfoundland and Labrador. Their offer was plainly and simply a test. Twenty nine minutes and 30 seconds later they heard my preparatory commands: "Ready AFRTS Slide; ready announcer." Twenty five seconds later they heard my commands of execution: "Show slide and announce," and since the station ID was made from the director's microphone, I heard myself say, "This is The Armed Forces Radio & Television Service, Sondrestrom Air Base,

Greenland." Thirty minutes later, another airman opened the refrigerator, offered me a beer and said, "Sarge, we heard you kicked butt in broadcast school; you're some kind of smooth dude." In their eyes I was ready to assume command.

My first shock came the next morning when I walked out of the barrack at 8 a.m., into complete darkness. Even though my orientations about Greenland informed me to expect extended darkness during the winter months, they didn't tell me darkness is a constant cover for almost three months. Conversely, during the summer months I should expect almost complete sunlight 24/7. It took about two weeks for my mind and body clock to adjust.

Another airman introduced himself as Ramsey. Following the untimely departure of the previous station manager, who was a NCO, Ramsey performed as manager while awaiting my arrival. He was very glad to see me, because he could now go home. Ramsey, like any GI after a few months of service, knew how to "get over" – to sometimes engage in non-criminal covert activity that is convenient for an immediate purpose.

One night when the thermometer dipped to almost 50 degrees below zero, Ramsey had a good night at the service club, but when he walked out the door to return to his barrack, the cold chill stimulated his imagination. He walked back inside and telephoned the air police to report a riot in progress at the service club. In quick order a force of policemen rushed in the front door to quell the disturbance. With perfect timing, Ramsey calmly walked out the rear door, seated himself in the warm police cruiser and drove himself home.

In addition to the 500 GI's on the base, our audience included the personnel who operated the Distant Early Warning (DEW) Line, a chain of radar sites dotting the polar ice cap that scanned the skies for incoming missiles, presumably, at that time, from Russia. It was at such sites that my training at the School of Aviation Medicine prepared me to serve as a medic. We also served persons assigned as Danish military liaison, and approximately 300 Danish civilians. Most of the civilians were employees of SAS Airline. Sondrestrom was a refueling stop for SAS flights between Los Angeles and Copenhagen.

Managing the station was especially exciting, including supervising a different type of professional while also letting them teach me techniques they had learned in civilian and other AFRTS stations. During the months of January, February, and March, I advanced my knowledge and gained experience as the program host of every music genre, and improved my interviewing skills. Our team was some of the finest men any supervisor could hope to lead. Airman Gary Gabriel always signed off his daily program with this hope: "May Dame Fortune smile on you; and not her unmarried daughter." One night the unmarried daughter, Miss-Fortune, came with a frown.

Even before I could properly answer the telephone at approximately 1 a.m., on April 1, I heard the operator say,

159

"Sergeant Alexander, The Castle is on fire. A car is waiting downstairs to take you there." As we turned the corner and the building came into view, the entire roof was clearly ablaze. My only concern was whether Chris, the night announcer, was safe. Before the car could stop completely, I flung open the door and rushed into the building, searching in the dark and repeatedly calling Chris. When I felt drops of melted tar falling on my parka, I decided to exit. Fifteen seconds after I crossed the threshold, I heard the roof collapsing, and being aware that the giant tower on the roof might fall in any direction, I ran the fastest 300 yards of my life and finally collapsed behind a fire truck. Someone got out of the truck and asked if I was OK. It was Chris. He gave me a hug and promised to list me in the Guinness Book of Records as the fastest black sergeant, who, even in darkness, was so scared that I appeared whiter than the snow. Everything was gone, including a new transmitter that had only been used one day.

Later that morning I telephoned the Pentagon to announce the loss of the station and to ask for recovery guidelines following such a disaster. A colonel proceeded to tell me the history of AFRTS, and that this was the first such loss in the long history; therefore, there were no recovery guidelines. My comments to the colonel expressed disbelief and disgust that not even basic contingency plans were available to help me through this crisis. He allowed me to explode. When I finally regained my composure, the colonel spoke: "OK, so you're pissed off. You just lost your station, and we don't have any guidelines to help you. However, Sergeant Alexander, there's something in your voice that tells me you'll do your best, and I've got a feeling we'll hear from you again."

My crew assembled in the Base Commander's office to formulate our own recovery plan. Even though I had no clue where I would start, I promised the commander that we would do our best to restore service as quickly as possible. Furthermore, I was mindful that this was the first station in the history of AFRTS to be destroyed by fire, and as a historian, my record of the incident might eventually be used as an exemplar. Therefore, I also promised the commander that my record would include our successful procedures, but especially our mistakes. Before adjournment we all stood in a circle and held hands symbolizing our unity and trust in each other. We also bowed our heads, and though no oral prayer was offered, each man understood the gesture and knew we needed help from an authority higher than the Pentagon.

Within hours I did telephone the next higher military Division Headquarters. Because of the importance of the station, my request for an immediate $100,000 was approved without the need for much discussion and burdensome paperwork. One finance officer there told me, "You rebuild; we finance and keep records."

Fortunately my predecessors had placed an old but still useful radio transmitter in a shed near the chapel that was occasionally used to broadcast church services. There also was a microphone in the chapel. At the passenger terminal someone had jokingly installed a turntable for playing tropical island songs to welcome new arrivals. A team of electricians and engineers, led by a Sergeant McCloud, undertook the task of connecting wires, twisting cables, soldering components and installing switches.

While they worked, someone remembered that Sondrestrom was primarily a listening base with enough powerful radio receivers capable of listening to any radio station in the world. We tuned to WLS in Chicago. When I telephoned WLS and explained our predicament and asked for permission to carry their programming while we installed equipment, their next station ID sounded something like, "This is WLS, the Big 89 in Chicago, also serving our troops at Sondrestrom Air Base, Greenland."

Nine hours later Airman Jim Sleeman was given the honor of activating the microphone and saying, "This is the Armed Forces Radio." We all just sat and looked at each other, the look that you give and get from teammates when you win the first leg of a marathon.

News of our crisis was also broadcast throughout AFRTS, and after two days every plane that landed brought surplus records and equipment from other stations. Over the next few months we operated from a suite in the Bachelor Officer Quarters (BOQ), as a new team of engineers, trained to construct broadcast stations, came from Alabama and started construction in the building that had already been designated to replace the Castle.

Someone at Division Headquarters discovered that, according to a proposal introduced at least two years earlier to upgrade facilities, the station was to be relocated, and the Castle was to be deliberately destroyed – by fire -- to give the firemen a training exercise. The scheduled date for the fire -- April 1, 1965.

He Was Here. He Came on the Rotator

Most of the planes that landed at Sondrestrom brought men to begin a one-year tour of duty and mail to comfort those who had additional days to serve. When the plane departed, it was loaded with men whose one year tour had ended and mail to comfort and reassure the folks at home.   We called the plane the rotator. In 1965, it was our main link with our families, so every landing or take-off had base-wide interest.

As we approached Christmas day, the rotator had not flown our way for more than a week. For those who were still stateside and scheduled to begin their yearlong stay away from their families, the delay gave them a few more days with their loved ones. Those whose tour had ended were eager to get home for the holidays. The rest of us just wanted mail from home. During 14 years of active duty in the Air Force I had observed odd reactions among GIs when mail didn't come.   Now, 500 men were reacting oddly as the wait extended. Then a couple of days before Christmas we heard the roar of airplane engines. All base activity ceased. Shift workers who were asleep abandoned their beds, and we all gathered at the terminal and smiled again. There was a glimpse of the new arrivals, but our attention was on the cargo -- the mail bags.

We at the radio station ordinarily waited for the call from the postman, so that we could broadcast the four magic words:

"The mail is up." But on this day, there was no need for the announcement; almost every man on the base had followed the mail bags from the terminal to the post office. When the doors finally opened, we filed in to collect letters, cards and boxes. Some of us had multiple packages; some men had waited for nothing, not even a greeting card. It was the fate of the latter that inspired one of the most beautiful acts of brotherly love I've ever witnessed.

A spirit of gaiety temporarily warmed the below-zero air as we rushed to our barracks to open the new pouches. Suddenly, without incitement from anyone, the fortunate many looked at the unfortunate few and knew what had to be done. Without a word or hint of intentions we walked directly into a spacious day room, rearranged the tables into a buffet style setting and placed all the food packages in a long row that stretched from wall to wall. It was as if God said to each of us, "...this do in remembrance of me." Cookies, cakes, pies and a variety of other foodstuff were abundant. Everything was everybody's.

Later that night as we cleaned the area, someone was heard to say, "We sure did have a good birthday party for Jesus Christ. Too bad he wasn't here to enjoy it too."

Another voice corrected him. "He *was* here. He *was* here."

One Target – Many Shooters

In November, I was informed that my next duty would be supervisor of the information office at Kincheloe AFB, Michigan. My negative reaction was swift. Having been assigned to bases in cold weather for the past four years, Michigan was not attractive. I placed a telephone call to a special sergeant at Randolph AFB. A year earlier he and Colonel Tulin had made me a promise.

He explained how I was chosen for the Kincheloe assignment. Because of my multiple specialties, (Senior Medical Technician, Senior Surgical Technician, Senior Information Technician, and now Broadcast Specialist and Station Manager), I was a big target. When my name came up for reassignment, another specialty section quickly filled a slot that I was qualified to assume. But he promised to override that order and honor his and Colonel Tulin's commitments.

Approximately an hour later he called back with this message: "I have located one very special assignment for a Senior Information Technician at the Ballistic System Division at Norton AFB, California. But the general there hand picks all senior non-commissioned officers. Have you ever heard of a Major General Harry Sands?"

There was a brief silence before I told him that General Sands and I had met when he was a brigadier. Then I asked him to have the general call me. In a very clear voice the sergeant asked,

"Just for the record, you want me to tell the general to call you? That means you also want me to keep looking for another assignment for you."

Twenty minutes later I answered the telephone: "Good afternoon, this is AFRTS; I'm Sergeant Alexander."

There was a familiar voice that said, "And this is Major General Sands. Are you that same outstanding sergeant from Dow AFB that I met two years ago?" Then the dialogue began:

Sergeant: Yes sir, I am.

General: Are you still as good at your job?

Sergeant: I'm better now, sir, and it seems you got better yourself.

General: Tell me, Sergeant Alexander, why am I calling you, instead of you calling me?

Sergeant: Sir, in order for me to reach you, I must rely on the availability of an unclassified line from Greenland, through Canada, through Washington, DC, through Denver, and finally to you. Any segment could be busy, and I didn't want to keep you waiting. Now, on the other hand, all you had to say is: 'This is General Sands, get me Greenland.' That is what you did, right, sir?"

General: Alexander, that is just so much bullshit, but you packaged it well. How would like to come work for me?

Sergeant: How long do I have to think about it, sir?

General: You just did, and I'll look forward to seeing you in a couple of months."

On the morning of my departure in January, 1966, I took one last stroll around the station and reviewed what had been one of the most exciting of my 31 years. I knew that, like so many other places I had left, I would probably not pass this way again. Then, just before departing for the terminal I opened the microphone and recited the lyrics of Ian Tyson's song, "Four Strong Winds":

Four strong winds that blow slowly

Seven seas that run high

All these things that don't change, come what may

But our good times are all gone

And I'm bound for moving on

I'll look for you if I'm ever back this way.

[Excerpts from Four Strong Winds printed by personal permission of Ian Tyson and Slick Fork Music.]

THE ROCK
Sondrestrom AB, Greenland

THE CASTLE

Temporary radio control
booth after the fire

My Rotator

Sondrestrom SUN article
April 16, 1965

AFRTS Crew

It's a Long Story

Our reunited family departed Bangor and headed west to California -- away from the cold. One night we chose a motel in Missouri for a rest stop. After bedding down the family I took a stroll to the adjoining restaurant for a cup of coffee. As I entered I had to pass a Missouri State Trooper, whose seat was at the counter where I placed my order. He greeted me and asked the universal question of a person in military uniform: "Howdy sergeant, where ya from?"

I answered, "I'm coming from Greenland, en route to my next assignment in California." His eyes brightened, and he announced, "I've got a brother in the Air Force, and he's stationed in Greenland."

I looked carefully at his name tag. He had an uncommon surname. I made some rapid calculations. Even though there were two Air Force bases in Greenland, (the other being Thule Air Base), the odds favored a relationship between the sergeant I knew, William, who also shared the trooper's unusual surname. I promptly announced, "I left Bill last week."

Suddenly I was in the clutches of the trooper as he hugged me and loudly announced to the other patrons, "The sergeant knows my brother, the sergeant knows my brother Bill, and he just left him in Greenland." He then grabbed a chair and sat me down to a table, and with a grin wider than his trooper hat, he asked,

"Tell me how he's doing. Tell me how he looks. Tell me what it's like up there where he is. Tell me, tell me about my brother. Just wait until I tell Mama."

An hour later I returned to the room. My wife's eyes asked why it took so long to get a cup of coffee. I simply looked at her and said, "It's a long story."

Welcome Home

On a warm night in January 1966, we arrived at Norton AFB and took temporary residence in the base guest house. Early the next morning I set out to find a home for my family in the city of San Bernardino. My search of the newspapers guided me to a clean neighborhood near a school. As I drove into the driveway, the owner rushed out of the house and quickly removed the FOR RENT sign and fumbled with an announcement that the place had just been rented. Having enough experience with when the color of my skin determined acceptance or rejection, the man's conduct was a classic racial rejection. In a calm and deliberate voice I admonished him for disrespecting both me and the uniform I wore.

At another address I was greeted by a white woman who politely showed me a house that was adequate for our family. But she informed me that she had given another prospective renter until 10 o'clock to sign a lease. It was approximately 9:15. I left and drove to a nearby coffee shop to continue my newspaper search, still wondering if her announcement was just another rejection. At approximately 10:20, I decided to test the lady's sincerity.

Immediately upon hearing my voice she declared, "Sergeant, I promised to hold open the offer for another man until 10 o'clock. He hasn't called. Go get your family and bring them to their new home."

We settled as the first black family in the little community of Laverne, among a cluster of neighbors whose immediate outreach was to make sure our children felt welcome and comfortable. One of the first neighborly acts was performed by Mary, a middle aged widow who baked a batch of brownies, then walked across the street, took the children's hands and guided them to a feast.

I was ready for duty, but at no time during my previous 15 years of service did I have to pass armed guards to enter my workplace. Upon entering the Ballistic Systems Division, a sentry escorted me to the Office of Information to meet the Director, Lieutenant Colonel George Kent. I was selected to join him as the only other military person assigned to a staff of civilian historians, researchers and speechwriters. After a pleasant greeting and introductions to the staff, he placed a call and simply announced: "Sir, he's here."

He walked with me to the Command Center where I was first greeted by a chief master sergeant, the Command Sergeant Major. When we entered the general's expansive office, the commander approached me and gave me a very warm hand shake, then put his arm around my shoulder and said, "Alex, it's good to see you again. Welcome to the best outfit in the Air Force." At our last meeting I was a staff sergeant and he was a brigadier general. Both of us had received promotions, so he put his hand on my stripes and said, "You put on a little weight."

I gestured to his added star and said, "We both look better than before."

Then the chief master sergeant said, "OK, General, so let's put him to work."

I turned to leave, but the general grabbed my arm and announced, "We've got you now, so here's your first order. My first meeting of the month is with the guys who run this place – you NCOs. Now, Alex, at that monthly meeting you will sit next to me. You will remember everything that is said, and if I'm asked to do something and I forget it, it will be your fault for not remembering it."

I simply looked at my three superiors and declared, "I've been in this building less than ten minutes and the three of you have already teamed up on me."

They said, almost in unison: "Yep."

When I returned to my office there was a large banner which read, "WELCOME SERGEANT ALEXANDER."

CITATION TO ACCOMPANY THE AWARD OF

THE AIR FORCE COMMENDATION MEDAL
(FIRST OAK LEAF CLUSTER)

TO
JAMES E. ALEXANDER

Technical Sergeant James E. Alexander distinguished himself by meritorious service as Station Manager, Armed Forces Radio and Television Service, Sondrestrom Air Base, Greenland, from 1 April 1965 through 23 December 1965. During this period, a disastrous fire razed the AFRTS facility. Technical Sergeant Alexander, through outstanding professional skill, knowledge, leadership, and considerable ingenuity, established radio services within eight hours after the fire in an interim location. Through diligent effort and with makeshift equipment, he re-established complete AFRTS audio-visual programming in a new facility. This unique and distinctive accomplishment of Technical Sergeant Alexander reflects credit upon himself and the United States Air Force.

General Sands awarding
the AF Commendation Medal
with Oak Leaf Cluster

Personal and Special Deliveries

Colonel Kent was appropriately assigned as the spokesperson for this unit charged with developing the Minuteman missile. We immediately felt comfortable as a team. Within a week he walked into my office holding a roster with approximately 30 names. He said, "Sergeant Alexander, I like your writing style so much that I'm going to give you a crappy job that I don't want to do."

The civilian speechwriter rushed to block the door, and loudly announced, "Alex is about to get screwed. Guard the windows so he doesn't jump out and run away."

Then my boss said that the biographies of all senior officers at BSD needed to be updated, but some officers always found excuses to avoid sitting for an hour interview. So he said, "Maybe they'll listen to a tech sergeant."

I said, "Sure they will. I'll inform them that their cooperation is essential, otherwise I'll write so much bullshit that they will retire trying to set the record straight."

The BSD building covered an entire city block. Couriers rode carts to shuttle documents among the far-flung offices. On June 3, 1966, Colonel Kent gave me an envelope addressed to a colonel in the office farthest from mine. Under the addressee's name was the notation: PERSONALLY DELIVERED BY TECHNICAL SERGEANT ALEXANDER. That ruled out the couriers. Upon receiving the envelope the officer quickly grabbed his coat and told me to follow him to the Office of Personnel. We moved swiftly, and as we arrived at the office door something very unusual happened: he knocked.

The door was opened by another officer -- Major General Harry James Sands, Jr., who escorted us to a room where approximately 25 persons waited around a large cake adorned with icing in the form of chevrons and lettering that read: CONGRATULATIONS: MASTER SERGEANT ALEXANDER." General Sands simply gave me a copy of promotion orders and said, "Alex, you deserve the extra weight. It's a pleasure serving with you."

Three months later, in September 1966, I was the recipient of a personal delivery. Sergeant Bill Harvey, Colonel Tulin's assistant at DINFOS, telephoned me and got right to the point: "Alex, remember when Colonel Tulin asked you to go to Greenland, he also said he owed you a big one. Well buddy, its payback time. We are inviting you to come to DINFOS and join the faculty in the Department of Radio/Television." Again, I stood motionless, but mindful that he had just given substance to Sergeant Robinson's promise: "Always do your best work, because everybody's got a ladder, and folks who are climbing will invite you to join them and add your muscle." Still, I immediately declined.

While I served in Greenland, DINFOS moved from New York to Ft. Benjamin Harrison, near Indianapolis, Indiana. I had less than five years remaining before retirement, and I anticipated a lengthy assignment at Norton. Furthermore, I wanted to finish college before retiring, and I had already explored taking classes at nearby University of California at Riverside, and the University of Redlands. Bill informed me that Indiana University and Butler University had campuses in Indianapolis. He also reminded me the DINFOS assignment was a four year tour, with the fifth year being my option. Therefore, he properly calculated, "This could be your last assignment." He observed my hesitancy.

Bill resumed and spoke slowly. "Alex, we want you here, but we'll understand if you don't come. Now, what I'm about to say is unrelated to our invitation." He again hesitated before disclosing an alternative. "I just saw the Vietnam assignment roster. Randolph is preparing orders for you to report to Pleiku on January 20, 1967."

My only response was: "What else will I teach, and when do I start?"

Chapter Seven: NEW VISIONS ON THE HORIZON

The Defense Information School (DINFOS)

Judy and the children said goodbye to me at the train station in San Bernardino, as I elected to travel alone by train to Indianapolis. My tour of duty at DINFOS would likely be my last military assignment, and I chose to take the long ride to contemplate much longer range schedules for my family and for a post-military life. There were new visions on the horizon. I needed to control the perspective and focus.

When I reported to Colonel Tulin, he was so proud to declare: "Alex, when I asked you to go to Greenland, you didn't hesitate, and I promised to take care of you. This is payback." He then ushered me to another office to meet another person. Standing with outstretched arms was Mrs. Christy. She had been informed of my arrival and wanted to give me a personal greeting.

Before we embraced I immediately asked, "Mrs. Christy, please tell me you didn't later discover any pictures out of place." It had been two years since she loaned me the family albums to complete my broadcast assignment, and I remembered that she had a good memory and that she took no prisoners. Colonel Christy then joined us, and the three of us stood there for a brief reunion, holding hands.

Within a month the family arrived at Fort Benjamin Harrison. To expedite our reunion we accepted a two bedroom apartment, with the understanding that the first larger home would be ours unless it was assigned to a higher ranking noncommissioned officer. Two months later I was informed through the NCO grapevine that a lower ranking sergeant was being given the larger apartment. I also was informed by the housing officer that his family was larger, and only the Post Commander could change the allocation. Post Headquarters was my next stop.

DINFOS was staffed by members from all military branches. Serving in joint-service units, on any military installation, requires all parties to make adjustments. On Air Force bases, eligibility for housing is according to rank and date of rank.

The commander explained that the sergeant who was getting the home had six children. I listened politely, but as he spoke I remembered two incidents that would shape my response. First, during the competition which earned for me the title of NCO of the Half Year in 1963 at Dow AFB, a panel of senior officers asked if I, a staff sergeant with four children, should get a house before a chief master sergeant with no children. Second, I remembered the master sergeant who gave the orientation during basic training, how his posture was at an angle to expose his six master sergeant stripes. I assumed that same posture and gave the commander essentially the same answer I gave to the panel of officers at Dow: "Sir, you and I know that it is harder to get promoted than it is to make a baby. God bless the children, but I want the larger apartment." He smiled, and patting the eagles on his shoulder, he said: "I get your point;" as he lifted the telephone to call the housing office.

As we shopped for 1966 Christmas gifts, I also studied the schedule of classes at the Indianapolis campus of Indiana University. On the first day of class in January 1967, I took my seat among the evening student body. Later that year I expanded my schedule to include classes at Butler University. Fortunately, spending my days in an academic setting as a teacher helped me to mentally transition to the role of student in the evening. Even more important was the support of Judy and the children, who understood that we all had a role to play, and at this time of our lives, my character was that of evening student.

Our children quickly adjusted to their new surroundings. Somewhere between the ages of 7 and 8 Kenneth became an entrepreneur. He scooped tadpoles from a pond behind the house, put them in a small jar with water, and sold them for a dime. When I reminded one customer, a lieutenant, that he was in fact buying "misappropriated government property," he rationalized that at his court-martial he would plead his unwavering support for budding capitalism. Their schools were first rate. James Christopher's fellow students elected him their Student Body President during his 7th, 8th and 9th school year, and his 10th grade classmates tapped him as their Class President. Joycelyn received kudos in the Indianapolis Star for her stellar job as a newspaper carrier. Dorothea, a preschooler, watched and took mental notes. Judy kept our home and all of us together.

Teaching at DINFOS with other highly qualified members from all branches of the armed forces was absolutely delightful. It was the ideal assignment at anytime, but especially at the end of a fantastic career. For the next three years the pattern was work, school, and even part-time employment. Almost every broadcast instructor who wanted part time employment for extra money or career development found it in Indianapolis. Someone noted that at 11 a.m., on Sunday, a DINFOS broadcast instructor was in the radio booth or in the television control room of most Indianapolis stations. I was a part-timer at the classical music station WAIV. One month after playing the music of Mozart, Tchaikovsky and Mendelssohn, the station was sold to an owner who immediately changed the format from classical to Soul. On the last day of the classical format I hosted a program and played three hours of Richard Wagner, my favorite composer. Then, at midnight, after delivering for the final time the required notice of a format change, I put a new record on the turntable for the next announcer. It just seemed natural that the new format and time of day dictated the title of the first song: *In the Midnight Hours,* by Wilson Pickett.

My contacts within the Indianapolis civilian community began to multiply. One day on a golf outing with an administrative assistant to then U.S. Senator Birch Bayh, D-Indiana, I was told to expect a call from Steve Scott, an executive at WFBM-TV. Steve did call and offered me the job of replacing him as host of the weekly television program *Job Line*. Each Saturday, the station presented a half-hour program, in cooperation with the Indiana Department of Labor, which offered listings of available jobs and training. Although I had not seen *Job Line,* I accepted the invitation.

When I arrived to videotape the fourth program, Eldon Campbell, the General Manager, greeted me and said, "You are worth watching. Keep it up." Shortly thereafter; as I drove home from another evening class, I saw a billboard advertising *Job Line*. It was one of several placed about the city, and they all bore my picture.

With DINFOS Instructors, SFC James, LCDR Bradford, Capt. Olson - 1969

DINFOS Instructor 1968

On Air Promotion

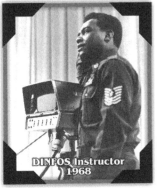

DINFOS Instructor 1968

Billboard Promotion

The Constant Pursuit for Education

SIX MORE NAMED FOR STUDY WEEK

SOUTH RUISLIP — The names of six additional students chosen to attend the University of Cambridge short resident course in international relations at Madingley Hall, Cambridge, March 26 through April 2, were announced this week by Dr. Donald Van Cleve, director of Third Air Force education and libraries division.

Van Cleve listed the six students — who will bring the total attending to 26 — as A/2C Arthur H. Pearson, Alconbury; 1st Lt William P. Suiter and Capt James G. Franklin, Upper Heyford; Capt Robert T. Davis, Greenham Common, and Capt Morris J. Ward and Maj John E. Delap, High Wycombe, Pietrek, Croughton; SSgt Hosea A. Phillips, Denham.

Capt Lucius F. Sinks, CWO James Marlatt, A1C Stanley L. Beard, Lakenheath; Maj James F. Sullivan, Capt Lester W. Krushat, SSgt Rigoberto Pinto, MMS detachments; Capt Bert Podell, Mildenhall; Maj Milton O. Freeman, Jr., Capt Joe Downs, Sculthorpe; 1st Lt Harry G. Perkins, Lt Col Rodericke McCaskill, Capt Glenn W. Mayer, Maj Edward B. Parsons, MSgt R.L. Zimmerman, SSgt James Alexander, South Ruislip.

Capt Evans Kranidas, TSgt Wayne Evert, Wethersfield; 1st Lt Richard A. Maxwell, 1st Lt Robert M. Stiffler, UK AACS Region; Maj George G. Fisher, Upper Heyford.

Study at Cambridge

In The Service
Works On Degree

EDITOR'S NOTE: Information for this article is supplied to the Times by the hometown information bureaus of the various branches of the armed forces.
BY TIMES STAFF WRITER

M. Sgt. James E. Alexander has been granted a 12-month leave of absence from the Air Force to obtain a degree at the University of Indiana.

Son of Mrs. J Katherine Johnson of Valdosta, he is currently serving on the faculty at the Defense Information School as a noncommissioned officer in charge of the radio-television department. He is to work toward a baccalaureate degree in broadcast management and a master or arts degree in mass communications.

After graduation from Dasher High School in 1951, he entered the Air Force. Except for a four-year period when he was unable to participate in the off-duty education program, most of the evenings during his 18 years of services have been spent in college classrooms.

He is to study as a full-time student from June 1969-June 1970.

Study at Indiana University

IU Student, 1970

In recognition of meritorious service

THE DEPARTMENT OF RADIO AND TELEVISION OF INDIANA UNIVERSITY

awards this certificate of excellence to

James Alexander

for outstanding achievement in

Radio & Television

during the Academic Year of

1969-70

Chairman
Department of Radio and Television

Dean
Arts and Sciences

IU Graduation, 1970
age 35

Indiana University
College of Arts and Sciences

To all who may read these letters, Greeting:

hereby it is certified that upon the recommendation of the Faculty, the Trustees of Indiana University have conferred upon

James Edward Alexander

the degree of

Bachelor of Science

in Radio and Television

in recognition of the fulfillment of the requirements for this degree. In Witness Whereof, this diploma is given at Bloomington, Indiana. Dated June 8, 1970.

Right of Way to Graduation

Sometimes there are two reasons for selecting a certain fork in the road: one, because the pathway can be easily traveled; the other, because you must take the passage that is the only way to your destination. In 1969 the calendar dictated my way home.

On a Monday morning in January 1969, I donned my Air Force uniform and drove from Indianapolis to Indiana University at Bloomington, carrying transcripts, certificates, performance reports, commendations, and any other support, both academic and military, to explain why I was wearing the rank of a master sergeant. I didn't know how many of my credits from various military and civilian schools were transferable to IU, so I drove and prayed; remembering the words of my grandmamma: "Don't expect God to come every time you call, but He'll come when you really need Him. It's also a good idea to help your self before He comes."

The place to start at IU was the Office of Admission. My entry into the office was closely followed by another man. When I asked the receptionist to direct me to someone who could help me determine my status, the man said, "That would be me. I'm Winford Wimmer." He directed me to his office, and after a brief review of the volume of papers to be evaluated, he politely told the receptionist: "Please reschedule my appointments for this morning; Sergeant Alexander has been on a long road getting here. Those six stripes say he's earned some of our time to let him know how much further he has to travel."

The Air Force offered a special incentive for members to upgrade their education. Upon accumulating enough credits to complete requirements for a degree, including Ph.D., eligible members could apply for a one year education leave of absence under a program appropriately called *Operation Bootstrap.* During the past 13 years I had attended countless highly structured military schools for courses in medicine, management, journalism, and broadcasting. Off duty, I travelled to classes by car, train, the *Tube* (London's underground), by bus and bicycle. And since most of them were evening classes, I also missed so many sunsets and chances to say good night to my children before their bedtime. They and my wife Judy supported me through every course.

After more than two hours of researching and calculating my credits, Mister Wimmer rose and simply said, "Sergeant Alexander, go and request your leave of absence under *Operation Bootstrap* from May 1969 to May 1970. You will leave as a graduate of Indiana University." I thanked him and subdued my excitement as I calmly walked to my car. And then I remembered Mama, and before starting the engine, I said a prayer of thanks and cried.

My request for the leave of absence was temporarily refused by the assignment section at the Pentagon, which stated that a one year replacement for me was impractical. But Colonel

Christy, as Commandant, sent a terse response which included a reminder that DINFOS was *his* command, and that any void during my absence would be filled – even if he had to personally fill it. It was hard to argue with a guy who went AWOL from his hospital bed to stand with his buddies during the Battle of the Bulge in WW II.

In June 1969, at age 34, I joined thousands of students on the campus of Indiana University, Bloomington. Most of them were not yet first graders in 1951 when I promised myself to one day join such an assembly on a college campus. My next stroke of luck was an introduction to Richard "Dick" Yoakum, a legendary professor of journalism and broadcasting.

Professor Yoakum called me into his office and told me how I would spend my last year in his department: "OK Alexander, at DINFOS, you have been teaching about six of the fundamental broadcast courses that are required for graduation from IU. So, master sergeant, schedule yourself to take the final exams in those courses; then you'll have time to help other students." Yoakum then called in another student, Alan Pearce, an Englishman who held bachelor and master degrees from The London School of Economics and Political Science, and The University of London. Alan was completing studies for a doctorate in business and telecommunications from IU. Yoakum gave us one of his trademark grins and said," Gentlemen, you're both TAs (Teaching Assistants), so go organize the newsroom."

For an entire year I was free to concentrate on a broader range of disciplines. Working and studying with Dick Yoakum and Alan Pearce capped that most exhilarating academic experience.

From my home in Valdosta my mother frequently asked about my studies, and she gave me another nick name: "Professor." And my sister Odessa, who taught me the alphabet, also asked about my progress. Both of them deserved to share the graduation ceremony, and in June 1970, they took their first plane rides to Indiana.

An Ugly Excuse Negated

In April 1971, two months before my military retirement, Eldon Campbell asked me to come to his office at WFBM. He was aware that much of the discussion in the broadcast industry at that time focused on the dearth of black participation, especially in management. Eldon was one of the giants of the industry, a person whose mere suggestions caused other broadcasters to take notice.

As a manager he knew that it was the technicians and administrative staff who kept the stations on air, but it was the managers in the boardrooms who selected the employees decided what audiences heard and saw. Too many broadcasters during that time excused black appeals for inclusion at the managerial level, citing "inability to find blacks with management level broadcast skills or potential." It was an ugly excuse, and Eldon rejected it. Instead, he focused on identifying persons with management skills in other industries, rightly reasoning that good managers would likely be good managers in broadcasting. He had heard me mention Denver as a possible city for relocation.

When I arrived at his office, he suggested that I sit, listen and observe. He placed a call to Hugh Terry, General Manager of the KLZ Stations in Denver; sister stations to WFBM, both owned by Time-Life Broadcasting. Eldon was direct: "Terry, I'm going to send James Alexander out to visit you. At the end of June he'll be 37 years old and retiring from the Air Force. For almost five years he's been teaching broadcasting at the Defense Information School, and he has on-air experience in both radio and television. Furthermore, he has years of management experience as a senior non-commissioned officer, and get this Terry, he has a degree in Broadcast Management from Indiana University." And, looking over at me sitting quietly, Eldon added: "Terry, the last time I saw him, he just happened to be black."

Terry's quick reply: "It sounds like he's either going to stay there with you or come to me. Has he got a twin brother?"

"...and four to go..."

On the night of June 30, 1971, after having turned in the keys to our house on base, our family sat in a motel in Indianapolis awaiting the end of the day. There was a noticeable calmness in the room. Each of us could almost feel each other's pulse, and each beat seemed synchronized with the second hand clock that ticked off the final minutes of an era.

At the end of the many courses I had taken and before departing from places that I would not likely visit again, I stopped momentarily and reviewed what I had learned and who had added to or borrowed from my presence. On this, my last day of military service, I sat quietly and glanced over my shoulder to recollect some significant persons and places, situations and circumstances that brought me to this day. Joycelyn noticed the far-away look on my face, and she came and sat close to me.

Two decades ago I left Valdosta as a 17-year-old boy on a journey into uncertainty on unmapped forks in the road. Almost immediately, I faced a horrible truth as Sergeant Hall's modest request for information from the library exposed my academic deficiency. But, that painful experience drove me to a spot on the parade field where I vowed to return, on another day, as a different person. I selected the medical corps, where many of my co-workers were educated professionals who introduced me to new visions and interpretations of life. I remembered Sergeants

195

Robinson and Perry. Both men died on active duty, but not before they enunciated some standards and techniques for good citizenship and service.

While I was still a boy I took a wife, and become a man, and we had become parents of four healthy wonderful children, beginning a new generation.

Some events which at first appeared to be simply fortuitous energized me into directions that could only be orchestrated by God. Such was the day I gave Sergeant Nick my pledge of support for his family, and how, a few years later he remembered my gesture and selected for me a super passageway to a better life. It was in England where fate channeled me to a most un-military style program called *On Target* that activated dormant talents and ignited in me a rebirth for new directions. Thereafter, everything that happened in Maine, Greenland, California, and Indiana, could be traced to that genesis.

Just a few minutes before 2400 hours the anticipation electrified the room, so I telephoned the military post and requested to be signed out. The Charge of Quarters (CQ), a non-commissioned officer who maintained the log for such purposes, reminded me that it was "Still too early to sign out on leave." I calmly informed the sergeant that his entry would change my status to Master Sergeant Alexander, James E., USAF, Retired. He honored my request and thanked me for my service. I slowly replaced the receiver, and gave thanks for my blessings.

There was too much adrenalin in the room to sleep, so we decided to leave immediately. We huddled and, as usual, asked God to travel with us, not only back home to Valdosta, but to other destinations in our new lives. My itinerary would include a place to keep a promise: the parade field at Lackland AFB.

It was Dorothea who initiated our final charge. She opened the motel door and started the nursery rhyme: "One for the money
.... Two for the show
.... Three to make ready…
We dashed to the car, and as we drove in the direction of a new finish line, our voices blended: "And four to go."

Alexander, James E.
MSgt, USAF, Retired
age 37